More
AWESOME CLIENT EVENTS!

More
AWESOME CLIENT EVENTS!

10th Anniversary Edition

Rod Burylo

Cover and Interior Design: Adina Cucicov, Flamingo Designs

ISBN: 978-0-9878534-0-0

First Paperback Edition: November 2011

TABLE OF CONTENTS

INTRODUCTION

Why would anyone write a book about client events? Perhaps an event planner would write a book about client events. Perhaps an event planner trying to drum up some business would be a candidate to write such a book. But why would a financial advisor write a book about client events?

This was a question that I was asked on a number of occasions ten years ago when I first divulged to a select group of friends and associates that I was writing a book about (given my professional work) such an unlikely topic. I remember distinctly telling my brother-in-law (who, rather ironically, is a very successful caterer and business person in the event planning business) while we were enjoying a relaxing swim at a pool in San Francisco.

"I am writing a book", I said, trying to sound matter-of-fact. "It's called *Awesome Client Events*".

"Really?" he asked somewhat disbelievingly, as if to suggest that it should really be *he* writing the book, "why?"

I don't recall exactly how I answered his question. Perhaps, I was not sure "why". After ten years worth of opportunity to reflect on my motivation, I think that I have an answer.

Awesome Client Events was my attempt to offer a bit of direction and encouragement to other struggling professionals and business owners who, like I had been, were working hard to be more successful. I expected that the audience would be made up of those who were already enjoying *some* success with practices and business activities, but who were also keen on taking those practices and businesses to the *next level* of success. I even imagined that there would be some readers who (also like me) wanted to be more than successful; they wanted to be exceptional and outstanding in some aspect of their profession or business.

I did not then, and do not now, think that there is any one strategy that will produce success with certainty; client events, no matter how awesome they might be, are not likely to be the only factor behind a successful business, and such events are certainly not likely to be the only means by which unusual success can be produced.

Yet, having had the opportunity to interview a number of top-performing professionals, from a variety of professions and locations, and having had the opportunity to replicate their efforts in my own business (often with surprising results), and having had the opportunity to teach and coach others to apply these ideas in the creation of their own success, I can attest with great confidence that awesome client events can be an extremely significant factor behind the creation of a truly exceptional business or practice.

Indeed, the implementation of a program of awesome client events is one of the very few strategies that can be broadly applied across various business activities, and by various practitioners, with no special skill, training or designation. I would even go so far as to suggest to anyone entering a competitive industry or profession that, if they were to short-list the skills or strategies that one must have to succeed in that industry or profession, "client relationship building through awesome client events" should most definitely be on that list.

My interest in sharing this message, and providing some direction and encouragement in the form of a book, was fostered primarily by the encouragement and direction that I had received from the numerous professionals that so generously shared their stories of struggle and accomplishment. Many of them had faced some challenges as they built their business, but eventually figured out a thing or two that made all the difference in taking that business to a higher level of success. Moreover, this sort of generous mentoring had been a prominent aspect of the corporate cultures (Royal Bank, and, especially, Investors Group) in which I had spent my formative years in the highly competitive industry of financial services, and in which was nurtured my own innate predisposition towards teaching.

"I have been interviewing some top-performing professionals, from various professions, in a wide variety of locations", I told my brother-in-law, as we continued to bob in the pool, "They all host awesome client events as part of their business".

"Why would they do that?" His curiosity was rising.

Another good question; that client events could be a solution to a complicated problem of business growth is very far from obvious and certainly requires some detailed explanation. This was another reason why a book on the topic would be worthwhile: a medium with ample opportunity to explore not only *how* client events could be made truly awesome, but *why* anyone would bother to do such a thing in the first place.

There is considerable benefit to the writer, as well as (hopefully) the reader, of going through the effort of detailing the *how's* and *why's* of some fairly abstract ideas (such as *success* and *relationships)* into words and sentences. One does not truly know what one knows about a subject until that knowledge can be clearly expressed to others in a way that not only informs, but motivates. Writing, therefore, is an exercise that may ultimately benefit the writer far more than the reader.

"I'd like to interview you as well," I said, "You've been a great source of ideas for me. How would you like to share your expertise with others?"

My brother-in-law beamed with delight.

So for me, writing *Awesome Client Events* ten years ago (after struggling in the financial services industry for 13 years) was like taking a bit of a break on a long journey: a moment to reflect on the progress made, to take stock of what had been experienced, and to get a sense of the direction in which to proceed.

This brings us to a more pressing question. Why would anyone write a *second* book about client events?

Well, my journey as a business person has continued in some remarkable and surprising directions. I have continued to network with top-performing professionals—learning from their new experiences—and I have continued to apply the strategies related to awesome client events for the benefit of successful, entrepreneurial business ventures. Some of these applications and benefits have been quite unexpected: small business branding, team-building, recruiting, international speaking and training events, and more.

On this journey, I have also come to realize that the interests in, and challenges regarding, relationship-building may be universal. One of my most memorable speaking engagements, for example, was in Washington, DC, for approximately 400 high-achieving financial advisors. Their enthusiastic response to the presentation confirmed for me that that the challenges of professionals and business owners transcend borders, and the need for some helpful suggestions and strategies is genuine.

So much has transpired with awesome client events over the last ten years that I have even found myself increasingly hesitant about responding to inquiries (that still come very regularly) for copies of the book. There is *so* much more which needs to be said.

Indeed, there are a number of significant and far-reaching developments of the previous decade that suggest a growing importance of this topic. The ubiquitous reliance on technology for communications, and in ever-more abbreviated *bites*, for example, suggests the need for a counter-measure of more significant human interaction. As well, the ferocity of competition among businesses and professionals has increased—and in some very difficult times (especially in the financial services industry)—spawning the need for *meaningful differentiation*. Further more, with North American baby boomers getting ready to transition into retirement *en masse*, there will be a need for professionals and business owners to organize their business operations to allow for an effective exit, while realizing the *full value* of those operations, and establish a successor. Awesome client events may figure prominently in these developments.

While the key elements behind making client events awesome (participants, venue/activity, communications, and lasting memories), and the basics for pulling these elements into a replicable system, have not changed since the first book, the information and ideas associated with each element has expanded in some new directions: including media relations, travelling with clients, branding in the office/service environment, and the needs of managers and team leaders. A number of new event examples have been added, as well as an up-date on some of the previously featured top-performers, tips of how to be cost-effective, and a report of "Biggest, Most Common Mistakes".

It is my hope that *More Awesome Client Events* provides *more* direction and encouragement to *more* professionals and business owners which results in even *more* success. I am confident that, by going through this exercise, I will also benefit greatly; I expect that it will represent for me another opportunity to pause on this journey, reflect on the progress over the last ten years, take stock of even more experiences, and again get a sense of in which direction to proceed.

"I am going to re-write Awesome Client Events," I said to my brother-in-law the other day, "you know, it's been ten years since the first one".

He smiled again, but did not ask "why?"

PART ONE

1

ACHIEVING IN HIGHLY COMPETITIVE ENVIRONMENTS

Charles Darwin is often credited with the expression "survival of the fittest". However, it is commonly accepted that Darwin's view was not that the most "fit" survive, but that the "most able to adapt" survive. The ability to adapt is required during circumstances when the environment is changing (and often rapidly so), in which competition grows increasingly fierce, and the ability to develop some competitive advantage is rewarded.

In that you are reading this book, I hope and expect that you are a participant in some competitive environment. Perhaps you are a small business owner seeking to establish, maintain or increase your share of the market. Or perhaps you are a professional with your own practice—a lawyer, an accountant, a dentist, a chiropractor, a financial advisor, a realtor; or a manager of an organization of such professionals. Or perhaps you are a leader of a much larger business operation, competing at a national or global level against other significant business operations. Regardless of the size of your business activity, or the length or time that you have been working at it, there are some problems common to all participants in highly competitive environments.

The most significant of these problems is the tendency of participants towards homogenization and commoditization of their products and services; that is to say, over time, those operating in competitive business environments begin to provide products and services, with processes, and for client and customer needs, that are qualitatively indistinguishable from the peers with whom they compete. Or, in even simpler terms, we do the same stuff, the same way, to solve the same problems.

When we do what everyone else does, the way that everyone else does it, we will produce the same results as everyone else. This is, by definition, mediocrity. I find this to be ironic because I do not believe that most professionals and business owners are consciously seeking to achieve mediocrity; on the contrary, most of the professionals and business owners that I have met and worked with are very goal orientated, and (at least believe they are) in pursuit of a higher level of success. In fact, it seems that the ability to even become a professional or entrepreneur requires a considerable amount of determination and competitive spirit.

How is it, then, that despite a propensity towards competition and success, so many professionals and business owners find themselves in the realm of mediocrity?

Competition and Mediocrity

The easy answer to this puzzle is that it is a tautology: that most members of a group would be considered average by definition (with some considered to be above the average, and some considered to be below the average). Not only is this answer uninteresting and defeatist, it rests upon a very limited understanding of the notions of goals, competition, and success. So let us consider a much more helpful (and protracted) answer.

Products and services tend towards indistinguishable similarity because that is a normal part of their life cycle. Early stages of the cycle are characterized by the introduction of a new product or service, or a significant innovation regarding an existing product or service. If the new or improved product and service is successful, and attracts customers and clients, it will also likely attract competitors. Perhaps the competitors initially find some additional improvement that can be brought to the product or service, but, eventually, competitors find that no significant additional value or benefit can be added. Without an opportunity for disruptive innovation, margins decline, and branding activity becomes more prominent in an attempt to associate some intangible value with the product or service. At the end of the cycle, there is no qualitative distinction between products and services of competing providers.

Aspects of the financial services industry, for example, have been described by many as being in decline. By this characterization, it is meant that, despite how it might often appear to consumers, the industry contains many products and services that are qualitatively indistinguishable from one provider to the next. As a result, many professionals within this industry have been finding their environment to be increasingly competitive. I have had ample opportunity to discuss this state of affairs with financial services professionals (as an industry trainer and consultant), and have found that the majority are unable to describe what makes their (or their firm's) offering of products and services different from their competitors'. If *they* are unable to describe a difference, how can the clients?

To put it in Darwinian terms, a business owner or professional involved in a mature or declining industry could certainly benefit from the ability to adapt, and by which seek to be different from their competitors.

Another reason that products and services tend towards indistinguishable similarity is because of the people providing them. In many cases, professionals are simply not taught the finer points of business activities and, specifically, the delivery of their professional services; typically, they are *educated* about their profession (law, accounting, real estate, financial planning, dentistry, chiropractic, etc), and they learn specific revenue generating activities related to their profession (writing a will, filing a tax return, selling a house, creating a retirement plan, cleaning teeth, performing an adjustment). However, they are usually left to figure out by themselves how to attract clients, effectively deliver the products and services of their profession, and generate a profit, all in a highly competitive environment. Frustrations may become acute as practitioners come to realize that the years spent developing skills and gaining knowledge, do not *automatically* manifest into a satisfying and successful business. In the absence of specific training on how to accomplish this, a professional is often inclined to conduct some market research as to how others in their profession are delivering their services. A bit of peer assessment is certainly a good thing, but it may very quickly become a slippery slope with the result that competing professionals and business owners become duplicates of each other. This is such a common result that very clear and universally accepted stereotypes persist in the various professions.

Drawing from your own life experiences, take a moment to imagine the work environments of some common professionals and business owners. Recall the stereotype of a dentist office, for example; picture the waiting room, uncomfortable chairs, dated and tattered magazines, the dentists chair, the pictures of teeth on the wall; remember the sounds of the drill and the smells. This is easy for any of us to do, because of the remarkable resilience of the stereotype.

Each common profession and business has its own prominent elements supporting a stereotype: lawyers with board rooms and bulging book-shelves, accountants with precariously stacked files and reports, chiropractors with models of spines, financial advisors with stock market performance charts and sales awards on the wall, etc., etc. Professionals doing the same thing, the same way: mediocrity.

So, business environments become highly competitive (most notably) when an industry is mature, products and services are qualitatively indistinguishable, and professionals and business owners are delivering those products and services in extremely similar ways. In these highly competitive environments, the ability to adapt and develop some form of meaning differentiation can be extremely valuable in the pursuit of success, or even just to survive.

Purpose, Product and Process

Efforts towards such differentiation can be applied in three distinct ways; professionals and business owners can differentiate by *purpose*, by *product*, and by *process*.

Even in highly competitive and mature industries, average practitioners, with no particular financial or operational support, but with a little creativity and motivation, can achieve extraordinary success through an effort to differentiate by purpose, by product, and by process. An example of the application of this strategy of differentiation is demonstrated by one of my life's more memorable business ventures.

Canadians Retiring Abroad Ltd. was founded to bring a full compliment of skills and services to a very particular prospective client: one seeking to enjoy an international retirement experience. We (I and two other distinguished and entrepreneurial financial advisors) recognized a growing opportunity to help clients with a specific need or problem—a very specific purpose: retirement abroad. (While some of our colleagues were seeking to differentiate by specializing in elder planning, or divorce, or succession planning, we thought our topics were far more exciting!) The value we could bring to clients with this purpose in mind was considerable; they would need to know about non-residential tax planning opportunities, asset management and banking services, real estate acquisition, cost of living, lifestyle pursuits, and many other sexy (for financial services) topics. We also had a very interesting and rare opportunity (again, for financial services) to differentiate by product: since an aging population of non-resident retirees would need health care services, and since non-resident Canadians can lose the ability to participate in the Canadian health care system, we created an international group health care plan; the first of its kind created by Canadians and specifically for Canadians. Finally, we were able to implement some unusual (and very enjoyable) processes to present our value to clients: we launched a series of awesome domestic and international client events—which included venues such as sea-side resorts, cruise ships, and existing expatriate communities in Mexico.

Canadians Retiring Abroad Ltd was presented with the prestigious Advisor of the Year Award (in 2004), which brought a host of television, radio and print media attention to our business. I believe that this success resulted largely from the fact that our purpose, product, and process were simply *different* from other financial services organizations.

I sincerely wished that I had learned about competition and differentiation earlier in my career; it might have helped me avoid some very frustrating and demoralizing experiences. One such experience stands out from the rest, as it left me contemplating a career change! However, that experience ultimately put me on the path to a new level of success.

I was a slightly-better-than-average performing financial planner with one of Canada's leading financial services companies. I had developed a small and growing practice, and was becoming fairly well-known in my community. I felt reasonably successful and was enjoying the rewards of my years of hard work: with a great wife, two wonderful children, a nice home, memorable vacations, etc. Yet, I was also ready to take my business to a higher level of success. But I did not have a clear strategy on how to do that. So I did what so many others have done: I looked around at what my competitors were up to, and saw that many of them were building their practices by providing educational seminars on topics related to financial services. In that I had always enjoyed public speaking anyway, I confidently decided that seminars would be my means of becoming a top-performing advisor.

So I developed a couple of seminars, put my presentation material together, and began to market myself as a speaker. It wasn't too long before a great opportunity presented itself. I was invited to speak at an education conference for a few hundred teachers at Calgary's landmark hotel, The Palliser. I really thought that this would be my proverbial *big break*.

It was the kind of conference that you are likely familiar with: in the morning, attendees were obliged to attend a larger, *main stage* presentation, and in the afternoon they could choose from a number of smaller *break out* sessions. I was one of the afternoon speakers; so I was in competition with the other speakers to attract an audience. I was invited to enjoy lunch before my session, which was held in the ball room with hundreds of teachers. Of all the people I could have eaten my lunch with, I found myself sitting at a table with one of the other afternoon speakers: my competition!

Bruce Kirkby was the most obvious person in the room. He is unusually tall, ruggedly handsome and, at that time, sported a long pony tail. I would quickly learn that he had spent much of the previous ten years leading expeditions to remote corners of the globe (including Mt Everest), and had recently returned from a most arduous trek across the Arabian Desert...*on the back of a camel*! He had shaved off his bleached, sand-filled beard for the conference, and to begin to promote his new book chronicling that journey: *Sand Dance*. He had prepared a presentation which included many pictures (oh, did I mention that he is also an exceptional photographer?), as back-drop to his countless tales of adventure and danger. I wish I could say that Bruce was intolerably "full of himself"; but, unfortunately for me, he is also most likable. As we chatted, I started to become quite nervous about my ability to compete against this speaker and attract an audience.

After lunch I anxiously rushed to my break out room and prepared it for my presentation. At 1:00, I threw open the doors to welcome my attendees. No one was there. A few minutes later, a hand-full of guests reluctantly trickled in: apparently *camel boy* had run out of chairs! I mustered up some self-esteem and gave my presentation. It did not go well. No one seemed to care about what Rod Burylo had to say regarding some boring financial planning matter. Had it not been for the deluge of laughter spilling over from Bruce Kirkby's presentation room next door, I would have lost most of my guests to an afternoon nap.

It was a long drive that evening to my home in the country. I reflected on the events of the day, and with the setting of the sun, my thoughts became increasingly dark. I had been so certain that, as a seminar provider, I could achieve a new level of success. How could I have been so wrong? How could I, after all the planning and effort, have so misjudged my abilities? Perhaps I had no real aptitude or instinct for what it would really take to become exceptional in my profession. Should I change careers, or simply accept that I will be not more than merely mediocre?

In the Soto tradition of Zen Buddhism, there is a belief that enlightenment can happen suddenly. I think that such a moment occurred on my drive home that day; for when my thoughts were at their darkest, an idea flashed into my head. If people were not interested in (yet another) boring presentation about money, and, instead, would rather be entertained by humorous tales of adventure, then *that* is what I would give them. I would organize an event for my clients, and their friends and family, featuring our young adventurer, Bruce Kirkby. And with that idea, my life would indeed change.

The use of client events within the processes of my professional practice became my first success at establishing meaningful differentiation. Whereas differentiation by product and purpose can be much more difficult endeavors (and I fully appreciate that most professionals and business owners cannot simply *decide* to introduce a novel product, or to significantly change their services to meet a novel client need, or purpose), differentiation by process, especially through the use of client events, can be within the abilities of almost everyone.

So, client events became my adaptation strategy in response to a highly competitive environment.

RELATIONSHIP-BUILDING FOR SUCCESS

C harles Darwin understood the nature of competition very well. Those that are able to adapt, he taught, would survive. However, survival is not the only *goal* of competition. Success in the natural world is ultimately not measured merely by the ability to survive, but by the ability to reproduce and nurture, at both the level of the individual and the group, for the perpetuation of the species.

In the world associated with our business and professional activities we face considerable competition, but what, specifically, are *we* competing for? How do we understand and measure our success?

Success, in the simplest of terms, is the setting and achieving of goals. Some goals are so universal, (like the desire to have a comfortable home, earn an attractive income, be surrounded by a loving family, etc.) that when we describe someone as being *successful*, we usually have a pretty good idea what that means. In other cases, however, an individual's success is related to some very personal goals: like losing weight, learning a new language, or crossing the Arabian Desert...*on the back of a camel!*

We can increase the likelihood of being successful—of accomplishing our goals—if the goals we set have certain features. For example, it is often proposed that we should set goals that are S.M.A.R.T.: goals that are **S**pecific, **M**easurable, **A**ction-orientated, **R**ealistic and **T**ime-limited (or something like that). Of course, if success necessarily resulted from the setting of S.M.A.R.T. goals, success would be relatively easy to achieve. However, I learned at a young age that *goal-setting* and *success* is quite a bit more complicated than that.

Competitive Goals

One of Canada's most enduring, and enlightening, symbols of competition, success and failure stood for decades in front of Vancouver's Empire Stadium. As a teenager, I viewed this statue almost daily from a public bus on my long commute from the suburbs to a small private school in that city's tough *East End*. Winter on the West Coast is characterized by endless days of drizzle and haze which would lull me to near-sleep most mornings; the sight of the statue, though, would disturb my daydreaming and prompt me to ring the bell for my stop.

The statue depicts Roger Bannister and John Landy—two fiercely competitive runners. Each had managed to accomplish, what was for its day, a remarkable feat; each had run a mile in less than four minutes. On May 6th, 1954, Bannister ran a mile in 3 minutes and 59.4 seconds—setting a world record. This was bettered less than two months later by Landy, who set a record of 3 minutes and 58 seconds. In August of the same year, with the world watching, the two met in Vancouver to compete, and to determine who was fastest.

As the story goes, Landy and Bannister were running shoulder to shoulder throughout the race. As the two were nearing the finish line, Landy manages to establish a small, but definite lead; however, with just steps before the finish line, he decides to turn his head to look for his competitor, Bannister. As he turns, Bannister is able to pass him on the other side to victory. The statue immortalizes the look of pain on Landy's face as he realizes that, by looking for Bannister, and thereby compromising his focus and stride, he gives him the opportunity for success.

Why was Landy **un**successful that day? Did he not have a goal? Certainty he did: his goal was to be first to the finish line, to win the race, to beat Bannister. Was his goal S.M.A.R.T.? Certainly it was. It was very **S**pecific: to be first to the finish line. It was **M**easurable: one mile from the starting line. It was **A**ction-orientated: able to be broken down into individual steps. It was **R**ealistic: he was already the world record holder, with a time faster that Bannister's best. It was even **T**ime-limited: ideally, within four minutes. There must be something more to this business of success than merely being a competent goal-setter, or else Landy would have accomplished his goal.

One of the things that I learned from the story of Landy and Bannister is that merely setting goals, however S.M.A.R.T., will not assure success. This is because there are actually different types of goals that we set. For example, we may establish a *competitive goal*. These are the goals that we set that are such that, if we are successful, it requires or implies the failure of someone else. A race is an excellent example of a *competitive goal*; Bannister's success required Landy's failure. Indeed, *competitive goal* environments, by the shear number of competitors, often produce considerably more failure than success.

Another example of a goal type is a *positive goal*. These are the goals that we set that are such that, if we are successful, it requires or implies the success of another as well. I tend to associate these types of goals with the activities of professionals and business owners, and the delivery of their products and services. As a financial planner, for example, I had a host of personal goals: related to income, net worth, sense of accomplishment, etc. I came to realize that I could accomplish these goals, if I helped others achieve their goals of building wealth, establishing a retirement plan, etc. My success depended upon their success. Or a realtor's goal of selling a listing may match up with a couple's goal of buying a new home. Or an accountant's goal of filing a particular number of tax returns in a given season, and feeling good about his or her abilities as a professional to help others minimize their taxes paid, will match up with that number of individuals that have a goal of filing in a timely manner and with paying a minimum amount of tax. These *positive goal* environments tend to foster more success than *competitive goal* environments.

One can increase the likelihood of success by setting S.M.A.R.T. and *positive* goals.

There is yet another lesson to be learned from Landy and Bannister. In *positive* and *competitive goal* environments, participants interact, and relationships are formed. The nature of these relationships can be very significant in influencing the outcome of the pursuit of the goal.

In a *competitive goal* environment *competitive relationships* are formed. Since, in these environments, success for one requires failure for others, the relationships do not serve to support the endeavors of the competitors, but to undermine them. In some examples, such as with Landy, the competitors become the focus of attention, rather than the true goal (a finish line, for example). This is such a common phenomenon in *competitive goal* environments, that competitors often adopt a strategy of distracting the others (a taunt, for example) as a competitive tactic.

On the other hand, in *positive goal* environments *positive relationships* are formed. Distinctly unlike *competitive relationships, positive relationships* can be extremely useful for goal accomplishment. In *positive goal* environments, where one's success depends upon the success of another, participants can be very supportive. As stakeholders in each other's success, participants collaborate, and will even sacrifice some short-term, personal interest in the pursuit of some longer term, mutual interest.

A person seeking to retire early, might take some time to gather investment statements for their advisor, who would then use the information to create a retirement plan, for the benefit of the investor, and, when the plan is implemented, for the benefit of the advisor.

A couple wanting to sell a home may take their realtor's advice and have some painting and staging done, which will help the realtor present and sell the home, which will help the couple buy a new home. The examples are as endless as there are goals, products, services, providers and professionals.

Moreover, by the nature of this interdependence within *positive goal* environments, these relationships may become among the most significant aspects of our personal, business and professional lives.

If a person wants to increase the likelihood of being successful, it would, therefore, be wise to set S.M.A.R.T goals, which are predominantly *positive,* and it would be most advantageous to attend to and nurture the *positive* relationships that will arise.

Returning again to a Darwinian perspective, highly competitive environments require participants to adapt through differentiation in the pursuit of some goal. In the natural world, the goal is related to procreation and species perpetuation, but in our social environments, human competitors appear to have myriad objective and pursuits, with *positive relationships* figuring prominently.

Indeed, *positive relationships* figure *so* prominently, that I have come to accept that it is extraordinarily useful to think of the relationships, themselves, as the true goal of our competitive pursuits—especially within the realm of our professional and business activities. Let me explain.

If you have been a competitor in your business or profession for any length of time, you have very likely engaged in some form of goal-setting activity. As a trainer, manager, and then director, of one of Canada's largest financial planning firms, not only have I participated in a number of highly structured goal-setting activities, I have had the opportunity to assist many others with the exercise. Using S.M.A.R.T as a guide, the goals tended to be related to some very specific and measurable revenue generating activity: a particular amount of new dollars under management, or particular amount of insurance premium, or a particular number of mortgages underwritten, and the like. Other professions and businesses would experience something similar: a particular number of billable hours charged, of treatments performed, of houses sold, of returns prepared and filed, etc. However, it was **this** sort of goal-setting that made me only a slightly-better-than-average performer.

Some of you may have also engaged in a somewhat more advanced variation of this goal-setting activity: creating a mission statement. These are often used to conceptualize, or frame, the goals and revenue generating activity. Mine tended to be along the lines of: "I am in the business of...helping others create wealth", or "I am in the business of...helping others gain financial independence", etc. Again, this had not helped me to become a top-performer.

It wasn't until I gained a much better understanding of goal setting, and the incredible importance of *positive* relationships, that I was able to frame my activities to produce greater success. This new understanding came when I was able to change the priority of my attention from a pre-occupation with the revenue generating activities and topics of my profession, to a specific focus on the clients. This was actually part of the same Soto enlightenment experience that occurred after meeting Bruce Kirkby, which lead from a pre-occupation with a financial planning matters as a subject of a seminar, to a focus on addressing the true interests of the audience (for adventure, excitement, humour, etc).

Mission: Positive Relationships

The result was a dramatically different mission statement; I realized that I was really "in the business of attaining and maintaining awesome client relationships". If I could do that, then the clients would benefit greatly from my dedicated attention, products, and services, while I would benefit from their loyalty, repeat business and referrals: *positive goals* set and *positive relationships* attended to.

With this newly conceptualized mission to fulfill, I contacted Bruce Kirkby to arrange for him to provide a presentation to some of my clients. This would be my first awesome client event.

Bruce was genuinely delighted to be of service, and we quickly selected some suitable dates in the following autumn. It was a good thing that I did not procrastinate on securing Bruce's services; his book would become an internationally-known and award-winning best seller, he was becoming an increasingly sought-after speaker, and his speaking fee was going up fast. It was also a good thing that I had allowed ample time for organizing the event; I needed that time to learn a bit about how to host a client event.

My research on the subject began with a survey of some peers and closest competitors; I was surprised and, initially, distraught to learn that none of those surveyed were hosting client events. Perhaps I was on the wrong track. I recognized, however, that those whom I had surveyed were not top-performers in their field; they were, like me, mediocre. I decided to attempt to track down and interview some professionals that had been recognized as outstanding.

I was somewhat fortunate, in that I had been networking with various professionals and business owners from a wide variety of industries, and so had several resources on how to track down some top-performers. As I made contact, and arranged for interviews, I was excited to learn that all of those interviewed were, indeed, engaged in hosting client events. I was also very pleased to discover that these award-winning, and extremely successful, practitioners were quite generous with information and keen to share their stories.

I learned about a wide range of events featuring fun escapades, exotic locations, and famous authors, speakers and entertainers. I learned how these top-performers had turned a potentially frivolous activity into a featured element of their practice, and of their personal brand. Each of these top-performers seemed to have something in common: they were excellent relationship-builders. Were they fully conscious of this skill, or was it instinctual? Regardless, I would "borrow" the best of the ideas and combine them to make my upcoming event into something awesome.

As the "big day" approached, and the myriad details of the event were attended to, I could feel the excitement rising: not only among the clients, their friends and family, but among my business team, the community at large, and even the media. New relationships were blooming, and established relationships were enjoying a fresh spark; Bruce and I were getting along famously, and he would ultimately provide the forward for the first edition of *Awesome Client Events*.

Some of my colleagues and competitors were also taking notice, and becoming increasingly curious about the event. I was differentiating myself in our highly competitive business environment. Success from these efforts was already beginning to materialize: success realized, not yet in the form of new business *per se*, but in the form of client relationships becoming awesome.

SPINNING THE PLATES—OR THE CHALLENGE OF SCALABILITY

T he natural world is a stage on which the struggle to survive unfolds in relentless drama: on which change is constant and, therefore, so too must be adaption and differentiation. The performers are unable to rest.

In our businesses activities, the struggle to compete, adapt, differentiate, set goals, build relationships, etc, is also relentless and, at times, stressful. When I recognized the importance of initiating and maintaining awesome client relationships as a primary means to success within my professional pursuits, I did not fully appreciate the very special form of stress that would emerge; it is one thing, I came to realize, to start a relationship, but it is an entirely different matter to keep that relationship going over time. I became fully cognizant of this stress at (of all places) the circus.

I had been engaging in a bit of relationship-building with my two wonderful children and a couple of their friends by attending a travelling circus. After enjoying the usual fare of acrobats, clowns and "wild" animals, our attention was drawn to the centre ring: for the guy that spins the plates.

He begins by placing a plate on top of a pole, and then the pole is gyrated until the plate on top is spinning on its own. He then initiates another pole and plate. This continues until several pairs of poles and plates are spinning in succession, and seemingly in defiance of gravity. The *fun* really begins when the poor plate-spinner must go back to the first poles and plates, now starting to slow and wobble, to give them some attention, and keep them spinning, while still trying to initiate new plate-pole pairs. There is no rest, and, despite his frantic efforts and obvious skills, the inevitable occurs: a plate will drop and shatter. As unnerving as this might be to the performer, he continues; for there are plates and poles that still require his attention.

"That's me!" I thought, with a rush of sincere empathy, "I know that stress!"

Like the plate-spinner, after I had initiated a new client relationship, I would need to attend to that relationship with sufficient frequency and effort to keep it "spinning". As my business had grown, the number of relationships was growing with it, and I was experiencing considerable stress in maintaining meaningful client interaction and initiating new relationships. Plates were starting to drop. I was experiencing a significant problem with capacity: a problem that would have to be solved if I were to realize the level of success to which I aspired.

Time is a critical factor for the success of most client-professional relationships, and it may be the factor that is most likely to distinguish that relationship from others, such as a vendor-customer relationship. The cost (in dollars and time) spent on the acquisition of a client is covered *over time*, as the services are rendered. If the business is run efficiently, and the relationship remains strong, the client becomes more profitable to the professional, again, *over time*.

Similarly, most clients, I believe, will receive greater benefit from working with a professional (and many other service providers and business operators) *over time*. This is because many of these benefits (like financial plans, health improvement/maintenance regimens, risk management initiatives, succession strategies, etc) are in dynamic environments, requiring monitoring and adjustments, and unfold *over time*. Everyone benefits when the plates keep spinning.

Relationship Capacity

Unfortunately, many established business owners and professionals seem to have an easier time of starting new relationships than they do of keeping those existing relationships going (at least with something approaching the enthusiasm with which they began). When the plates start dropping, the natural inclination of many is to add new plates. However (and at the risk of asking too much of this metaphor), it takes less energy and attention to keep a plate spinning than it does to initiate a new plate: if the problem of capacity can be solved—getting to all the plates.

The capacity problem, when it comes to relationships, is an ancient one, and could very likely predate our species. Various scientific disciplines, through the study of historical changes in hominid skull remains and supposed correlations with brain size, functionality and tribe size, contribute to the belief that pre-humans developed in a particular fashion, as a particular adaptive response, to a particular change. Specifically, as the tribe size grew, our ancestors adapted to be able to manage a greater number of relationships.

In the simplest of terms, we developed skills at distinguishing friend from foe; or, at distinguishing those that would seek to benefit at our expense, from those that would seek to benefit as we benefit. In other words, we became increasingly adept at recognizing competitive goals and competitive relationships, relative to positive goals and positive relationships, in a growing population. History suggests that the increase in capacity to recognize and nurture a greater number of positive relationships is an advantageous adaptation. However, the evidence suggests that, based upon our current physical attributes, a typical professional and business person likely has the natural capacity to successfully manage only around 150 relationships (which is believed, by the way, to be not many more than that of a Neanderthal).

Therein lay our capacity problem. You and I may be attempting to manage many more than 150 client relationships, in addition to those countless other relationships known as partners, wholesalers, suppliers, stakeholders, family, friends, teammates, fellow parishioners, and on and on. Is it any wonder, then, that many of us feel that special kind of relationship management stress?

Unlike almost all other life forms, though, when humans face such stressors, circumstances where adaption will be rewarded, and our natural, physical capacities are reached, we employ our somewhat unique abilities as clever tool-makers; these tools, strategies, innovations, technologies, etc become the means by which we seek to overcome our limitations in the pursuit of our goals. When it comes to relationship building, professionals and business owners tend to adopt tools and strategies to accomplish two very specific objectives: to increase the number of client interactions and to achieve at least a minimum significance to that interaction.

In the pursuit of these objectives, a seemingly inherent difficulty becomes readily apparent: the greater the number of individuals that we attempt to have a meaningful connection with, the less significant that interaction becomes. Just getting to the poles will not necessarily keep the plates spinning.

When we are well within capacity, and managing a small number of relationships, our innate abilities and natural propensities (developed over millennia) are often excellent. We tend to know instinctually how to make a relationship meaningful. A common element is the sharing of a memorable experience or, ideally, multiple such experiences. I imagine that those that went to war together, and shared many terrible experiences, could feel a significant relationship bond over, perhaps, their entire life. As well, I believe this also explains why many feel a life-long connection with childhood and high school friends long after they reach the point that the only thing that they continue to have in common is that (often very brief) history.

I have seen a number of professionals and business owners, especially in the financial services industry, implement strategies for relationship building with this "bonding experience" or "shared history" principle in mind. The less creative will perhaps invite a client or two to a sporting event. The more creative will adopt a more personalized approach: perhaps, for example, after noting that the target client is about to experience a significant wedding anniversary, and remembering their mutual fondness for musical theatre, the relationship building professional arranges for excellent seats to an exclusive upcoming performance, attends with the clients, enjoys refreshments prior, and arranges for shared transportation. While the creative approach is significantly more likely to be an effective relationship building activity (for reasons I will explore more completely in the *Lasting Memories* section) than the comparatively uncreative approach, both will ultimately suffer from a similar difficulty; such would-be relationship builders tend to find the required costs and time to be extraordinarily prohibitive when attempting to multiply this effort across even a portion of their client base. More than a few, well-intentioned professionals have, in the time-consuming pursuit of better client relationships, ultimately negatively impacted another significant relationship: the one at home.

Scaling-up Relationship-building

This is what I call the *challenge of scalability*. That is, the professional cannot effectively increase the number of such relationship-building activities to the extent that it serves as a business-wide or practice-wide initiative, with a diminishing cost and effort relative to scale. This form of relationship-building strategy can quickly become neither cost-effective nor time-effective. Although the individual client *touch* can be significant, the number of clients so *touched* tends to be low.

At the other end of the potential relationship-building activities spectrum, there are a host of very familiar strategies employed throughout the professions, and by a wide variety of business operators, designed specifically to touch many clients, and in a cost-and-time-effective manner. I have witnessed the dramatic evolution of these activities over the last three decades.

My financial services career began when I accepted an offer to work as a stock broker's assistant in Vancouver in September, 1987. With those two wonderful children arriving prior to the completion of my undergraduate degree, and although I was well-prepared educationally for law school, it was clear that I needed to make some money. As I had never really thought about financial services as a career option, and lacking confidence that I had any particular aptitude for the work, I accepted the position already contemplating a contingency plan: becoming a teacher. A month later the crash of 1987 occurred, and my contingency plan was looking increasingly attractive.

The work of a stock broker, connected with the rather infamous *VSE*, in 1987, was a rather low-tech enterprise. Although large, desk-top computers had recently arrived to the office, they did little more than provide quotes. The trades themselves were still received and implemented by a cumbersome series of written, phoned and hand delivered communications. Information was most-often shared face-to-face, and it was the ability to gather this information and digest it into investment opportunities, that set the successful apart. I was fortunate in that my family was fairly well-connected in this business world, and, as a result, I was able to meet and learn from some very well-known businessmen of the day. They often met at our office and I was able to listen in on many of the meetings, except when their secured communications strategy was implemented: when they spoke Polish. I am not kidding. A few years later, I arrived at Royal Bank of Canada, and desk-top computers still had not.

Larger scale relationship-building activities reflected the resources and technology available at the time. In an effort to touch many, professionals and business owners mailed birthday cards, Christmas cards, calendars, and the like. Realtors stand out, in my mind, as notable in this regard; they became well-known for mass communications efforts featuring personalized pens and note pads. While other industries and professions were more likely to feature newsletters in their activities. Even the various periodic statements (and accompanying sundries) sent by financial institutions are a form of regular client touch.

Though many were touched by these activities, the significance of the touch was typically low. Communication efforts that attempt to say something to everyone ultimately tend to say nothing of any particular importance to the individual. Moreover, competitors often adopt similar (undifferentiated) efforts, and the recipients become deluged with unremarkable, unmemorable touches: getting to the poles, but without sufficient significance to keep the plates spinning.

These communications have simply become part of the ever-increasing cacophony that has come to characterize our modern lives, and the advancement of communications technology has contributed significantly to this deluge.

Now it seems that many humans are in a state of perpetual interaction. Cell phones, and other forms of personal communication devices, are omnipresent and ensure that we are constantly connected with our positive relationships; while, increasingly, we are attempting to expand that group through participation in, so-called, social networking web sites. Many of these on-line interactions are similar to the mass communication efforts of the previous, low-tech genre, in that they tend to say something to everyone and, in so doing, say nothing of any particular importance to the individual. There is, I believe, at least one notable difference between the two genres.

With previous efforts, such as the mass mail-out of Christmas cards, calendars, birthday cards, and the like, the senders perhaps did not really expect that, by that effort alone, they were building relationships. They knew that they needed to touch their clients *somehow,* and recognized that competitors were likely attempting to touch them as well; in the absence of any better idea, the generic, inexpensive and easy to systematize (by delegating to an assistant) mass communication strategies would have to do. The difference today—especially with the social networking sites—is that many of the participants really believe that they are building relationships.

This seems to be the sentiment particularly among young up-and-coming professionals and business owners. Not only have they grown up with technology, and seemingly embraced it unconditionally, in many cases they do not have sufficient years behind them to recognize the significance of the "bonding experience" or "shared history" as they relate to formation of long-term, exceptional, positive relationships. The key piece typically missing from these high-tech interactions, that would lend itself cumulatively towards relationship-building, is "face time". As face-to-face interaction has diminished in relative frequency, the subtler physical, facial, and inflective aspects of human communication, which are also considered to be instrumental towards meaningful interpersonal connections, have also become less prevalent.

While the number of people that we communicate with, and the frequency of those communications, is growing, the average significance of those touches is declining. Regardless, with advances in technology accepted as sexy and cutting edge, we and our competitors continue to embrace those media as providing inexpensive solutions to our relationship building needs, without considering whether or not they are truly effective. Perhaps it is felt that, if everyone else is relying on these communications strategies, they *must* be effective and, therefore, *must* be adopted: a slippery slope towards doing the same thing, the same way, for the same people in the pursuit of mediocrity.

Is there a solution to this challenge of scalability? Can the plate-spinner touch all the plates, and do so efficiently, effectively and with sufficient significance to keep them spinning?

A solution to this puzzle came to me as the planning of my first awesome client event was reaching fruition.

My financial planning practice was based in a small community just north of Calgary. With a population of approximately 20,000 (at the time), my choices for potential venues to host my event were few. The local theatre, with a full stage, box office, and seating for 400 hundred, was quite suitable—though much larger than what I thought I would need; I was hoping to have more than 100 guests, but, having not hosted an event before, I really had no idea what to expect. Having conducted some research among a net-work of top-performing professionals regarding their client events, I had managed to formulate and implement a communications strategy based upon their suggestions. As the date of the event approached, and RSVP's started arriving, I became increasingly optimistic that my attendance objectives would be met.

At the same time, however, some unexpected parties had taken an interest in the coming event. A local book store decided to support a pre-event book signing for Kirkby and his increasingly popular book, while the theatre manager decided to support the activity by creating and distributing some posters. The graphic design for these was then used as an announcement in a local newspaper, which prompted the editor to contact me in an effort to reach Kirkby for an interview. That interview, and large colour photograph, became a lead story, and the public began to make inquiries regarding my little client event.

With all that attention, we ultimately exceeded our goal of 100 guests by having a full house of 400. And that was just the first night! Moved by the extraordinary interest in Kirkby's presentation, I decided to host a second event the following night for the public. Fortunately, both he and the theatre were available, and enough tickets were sold for the second night (as the first night was free for clients) to cover the costs of both performances!

My memories of the event remain vivid. Guests enthusiastically poured into the theatre and prime seats were claimed quickly. As I provided the opening remarks and introductions for the presenter, the audience's anticipation was palpable. Kirkby's tales of adventure and danger, mixed with humour, supported by a slide show of his amazing photographs, and a hint of feel-good inspiration, was the perfect blend of escapism, entertainment and information. We were all having an experience together: an experience that would become an element of our shared history.

Not only had the event addressed the true interests of the audience (in stark contrast to my ill-fated attempt at the teacher's conference), but the size of the audience (over both nights) was truly remarkable. The event touched hundreds of clients, friends, family and strangers, and touched them with some significance. New relationships were being initiated and others nurtured, in a highly distinctive, cost-effective, time-effective, and (rather than stressful) very enjoyable manner.

I was getting to all the plates, and keeping them spinning.

MEASURING
THE IMMEASURABLE

"There he is *again!*" I called out to my wife, Anna, from the living room, where I was watching the local news. She rushed in, quickly fixed her eyes on the big-screen television, and her face filled with a smile.

"How does he *do* that?" I asked, with equal measures of awe, jealousy, and respect, "How does he manage to get so much attention from the media?"

Anna shrugged her shoulders, and joined me on the couch to watch the rest of the story: my brother-in-law, Chef Carlo, dressed in his kitchen whites and tall hat, was shown preparing and serving some culinary creation to a room of some well-dressed business types at some important event.

Carlo is gregarious and charismatic (in a stereotypical Italian sort of way). He is keenly passionate about food and people (or, more specifically, what happens when you bring the two together) which has helped him to achieve considerable notoriety and success. As an entrepreneur and street-savvy relationship-builder, he has molded a small, family run business, into a large and sophisticated enterprise. He has an unmistakable physical presence, and is often seen about town, driving his black Escalade and smoking a cigar. Yes, Carlo is the "Tony Soprano" of caterers.

Carlo, and his extended family that manage their business, are often featured on the local television and in the local newspapers. For some time, the frequency of these occurrences had both impressed and puzzled me. Since neither my brother-in-law, nor any of the rest of the Roma Catering staff, were celebrity athletes, or international speakers, or world leaders, or influential politicians, or captains of industry, or travelling performers, or notable philanthropists, or the like, I had difficulty in fathoming how they managed to warrant such attention.

"Yes, you are correct, Rod", Carlo began to explain to me, in between pulls on a freshly lit *Cuban*, "We are none of those people. But all of those people either use or participate in events. And that's what we do. So we get involved in all those things. Being in the news in one of the ways that I know that I am involved with great events."

Indeed, Carlo's services have long been associated with some of the city's premier annual events (such as the world famous Calgary Stampede, and the Sportsman Dinner—which features special guest speakers, like Pete Rose), as well as special events, such as high-profile AGM's, political gatherings, and charitable fundraisers. Of particular note, was their company's contribution to the success of a G8 summit—as commemorated in a proudly displayed letter from the White House!

Carlo's insight was recognizing that events are used by a broad range of people and organizations, in pursuit of a variety of agendas, and that his association with these would not only provide profit in the short-run, but it would (very cost-effectively) ensure an increasing profile and status of the company.

Through some of his generous mentorship, I also came to benefit from this insight, and I have applied the principles and strategies associated with awesome client events to achieve a wide variety of specific objectives (both for my benefit, as well as for the benefit of many others), and with some interesting variations on the relationship-building theme. In particular, I was struck by how Carlo could measure (at least in part) his success: by "being in the news".

Client Retention, Response and Referrals

How could *I* measure the success of my own relationship-building activities? Though I may know, intuitively, when a particular relationship is "strong", or "has improved", could I objectively measure changes in a relationship to determine whether or not a particular strategy, such as awesome client events, has true merit?

The approach I adopted, as I applied the event strategy broadly to various objectives, was to select quantifiable characteristics of my business. Initially, the focus was on client *retention, response,* and *referrals.*

Client retention provides the business person and the professional with the opportunity to gain a return from the cost and time spent on client acquisition activities. Since, with many operations, it typically costs more to gain a new client than it does to keep a client, effective strategies for client retention can be extremely valuable. Client retention is also a measurable characteristic, and is an indicator of the quality of relationship with the service provider. I (and many others) have found that client relationships last longer in correlation with the establishment of a practice/business culture of awesome client events.

Client response refers to the likelihood of a client responding positively to, heeding, or taking specific action based upon the direction, advice, and/or suggestions of the professional or business operator. The response may be in the form of following the prescribed regimen of a health professional, or implementing the tactics recommended by a lawyer or accountant. Generating the desired *response* from a client can be an interesting challenge; neither the credibility of the communicator, nor the quality of the advice or direction alone, will assure to result in action. (I gained some insight into this issue during my graduate studies as I was exploring the problem of *non-compliance*—patients not following doctor's orders—at Calgary's Health Science Institute.) In the financial services industry, for example, competition and consolidation has allowed for the opportunity for service providers to increase and diversify their product offerings; the number of products per client is a measurable characteristic, is indicative of a level of confidence and trust by the client in the provider, and correlates with the overall quality of the relationship. As with other professional and business activities, both the service provider and intended recipient can benefit when this communication results in action. I (and others) measured an increase in such successful "cross-sell" initiatives (responses) as a culture of relationship-building was developed.

Moreover, and in dramatic fashion, the number and quality of client referrals increased. While some may quibble over the true cause-and-effect relationship between client events and the increase in retention and response, the connection between events and referrals is unmistakable. This is because, as clients came to realize that the events were interesting, enjoyable, memorable and fun, and that future events would be the same, they would request (even insist) that their friends and family be able to attend. Such guests were, of course, introduced to the organizer (me, or a member of my team), and many were, in short order, eager to learn more about our services. They realized, from the very beginning, that we were different from their current service providers.

In addition to retention, referral, and response, other measurable objectives came to be associated with awesome client events as the strategy became more broadly applied, in particular with regards to *recruiting* and *team-building*.

Recruiting and Team-building

In more recent years, the focus of my business efforts has been directed towards growing an Exempt Market Dealership: a form of investment dealer. My partner and I had identified an emerging opportunity to participate in a quickly changing and newly regulated sector of the Canadian capital markets. The value we sought to bring to the sector included an independent review of alternative, primary market investments, as well as leading education for the public and professionals. Having completed a market test, proved the viability of the business model, confirmed the attractiveness of the value proposition, and established our points of differentiation, we were set to expand operations.

We recognized that the purpose of the expansion was to increase the number participants in our services, or, to initiate and maintain an increasing number of positive relationships. We also identified three distinct challenges with this pursuit, as we scaled-up our relationship-building: the urgency of our message, the complexity of our message, and the fact that we would be attempting to communicate that message to three distinct audiences. Awesome client events came to figure prominently in the solution to these challenges.

First, we felt some urgency behind our efforts—much more than should be chalked up to as merely the impatience of entrepreneurs. The intensity of our interest in the types of investments that we were reviewing, and the underlying assets, was in no small part due to the belief that the North American stock markets (and perhaps others) were poised to experience a significant correction. (The rationale for this position was presented in detail as a primary message of my

Move It or Lose It: Smart Money for the Next Score, written late in 2006, and being distributed in early 2007, and of a host of speaking engagements). As such, we wanted to communicate to as many of those people as possible, in as short of time as was practical.

Second, our message, which covered such far reaching topics as demographics, aging population trends, forces of supply and demand, influences of investor sentiment, alternative investment strategies, and the like, was relatively complicated. Moreover, we recognized that this message was rendered less palatable to some in that it was in contradiction with the many other messages from representatives of the large established media, and financial services industry. (In fact, portions of our communications effort were dedicated to explaining to our audience why they were unlikely to hear this message from some other sources.) We would need a communication effort that would allow for the message to be fully formed and fleshed out for the audience, and felt that the distribution of the book, alone, would not suffice.

Finally, we had identified three distinct audiences for the message— three distinct groups that would receive value from our services: end-user, or retail level, investors; advisors and other professional centres-of-influence; the manufacturer of the investments. We would refer to each of these as a form of potential client, but their level of sophistication, interests and agendas vary considerably.

Our dealership, Global Exempt Market Solutions, launched a series of client events as the means of quickly and effectively communicating a complicated message to a diverse, and (we hoped) large and interested audience. We leveraged off of my reputation as a speaker and award winning advisor, in conjunction with a promotion of *Move It or Lose It*, in an attempt to entice our various, potentially new, relationships to a keynote presentation. Members of the current investor group were eager to attend, often with friends and family, to receive relevant information from an objective source. Advisors from our existing network and their clients, as well as centres-of-influence that we had targeted as potential recruits for our firm, were encouraged to attend to learn about important and timely developments for their business. While current manufacturer relationships were encouraged to organize and/or sponsor the event, potentially new manufacturer relationships were invited to learn about our unusual, valued added model for distribution, and how they might benefit. During the events, we attempted to find that delicate balance with the delivery of the message: not so technical and promotional as to be boring or self-indulgent, but sufficiently complete and interesting to establish our differentiation and promote a relationship.

The results from the strategy have been both wonderful and measurable. Our success with growing the company, by engaging relationships of significant quantity and quality, is measured by the dramatic growth in the number of end-user investors and participating advisors. Having not merely heard a "pitch", but experienced our unique approach, manufacturers have been increasing interested in our services, and the contractual arrangements have been measurably more attractive. While the value to the investing audience is fairly obvious (improving their investment portfolios), the attraction for advisors and manufactures arises in part from some far less obvious objectives and needs.

The advisors and manufacturers recognize that they are in highly competitive environments. Whether or not they are fully aware of it, a reasonable strategy in this environment is to adapt, and pursue reward through differentiation. If they cannot differentiate on their own (through one or more of the identified categories of differentiation: purpose, product and process), they can seek to establish a relationship with those that can. The formation of suitable positive relationships *is* their means to differentiation.

Just as professionals and business owners seek to distinguish themselves in their market place for an audience of prospective consumers, end-users and clients, the managers of such professionals seek to distinguish themselves from other employers, companies, firms, practices, associations and other organizations for an audience of potential recruits, future partners, and myriad other human resource needs. For a portion of my own career, for example, I held various roles related to training, recruiting and managing for a large, national, financial services company. One of the challenges I had, when attempting to attract new advisors, was trying to articulate what made the products and services offering of our firm meaningfully different from a number of others in the industry (each of whom were also trying to communicate the same message, to the same audience, for the same purpose...and with the same challenges).

As a manager of a dealership, potential advisor recruits were my prospective clients; as such, they were invited to events. This was my opportunity to demonstrate our firm's unique value proposition, in terms of product, purpose and process, with the pitch: our competitive differentiation can be *your* competitive differentiation. The same strategy also attracted exceptional support staff, and higher-level managerial leaders: folks that wanted to be part of something different, with an unusual opportunity to offer value.

Since these many new relationships formed were positive (some interdependence related to accomplishing goals), we were keen to implement a strategy of awesome client events specifically for the benefit of those new recruits, managers, wholesalers, etc and *their* positive relationships. In other words, the events that attracted and initiated new advisor relationships to our firm would also be used to launch them to their clients, community, friends and family. Moreover, a culture of relationship-building through memorable events could be created to keep all these plates spinning.

Though attempting to apply the strategy of client events in the hopes of initiating and maintaining a broad array of awesome relationships, we are vigilant in the measurement of the correlating and readily quantifiable characteristics (retention, response, referrals, and recruits) as we monitor our growth. However, while our growth-stage operation capitalizes on this strategy, I have also consulted with organizations at different stages, and client events proved to be effective for other purposes: for a mature organization seeking to re-energize in conjunction with the launch of a new product/service, measured by client response; for a seasoned professional initiating a retirement and succession plan, measured by client retention; for a collective of professionals changing their sponsoring affiliate, measured by referrals; for a company reorganizing, and introducing new key personnel, measured by recruiting. Despite the differing circumstances, client events were employed as efficient, effective, scalable, and replicable tools to communicate differentiation for the purpose of building relationships.

Ultimately, awesome client events can come to attract the attention of a far greater audience than the organizer might initially expect: well beyond the myriad targeted existing and pursued relationships. As I learned from Chef Carlo, truly awesome events are noticed by, and reported by, the media—which suggests that the public can also be potential participants (much more on this in Part 2). From the example of his success, I have found that approaching the strategy of events with an ambitious relationship-building agenda, while tracking the measurable indicators of progress, can produce exceptional results.

SUMMARY

Many professionals and business owners operate in highly competitive environments, where there is a natural tendency towards imitation and unremarkable similarity among services. A vicious circle ensues: as competition grows, we become increasingly interested in our competitors, imitation continues, and competition grows.

In such an environment, participants can benefit through adapting a strategy that pursues differentiation from these competitors. While the target of such differentiation ideally includes each of *purpose, product and process,* the later is typically the most readily available option to address.

There are risks inherent in the pursuit of, and realization of, differentiation—for not every adaptation results in an advantage. The risk, however, is necessary if mediocrity is to be overcome, and the reward of exceptionality and success achieved.

Success, itself, requires more than merely effectively setting goals.

The likelihood of success increases when, specifically, positive goals are emphasized, and the resulting positive relationships are cultivated and nurtured.

Relationship-builders are hindered in these pursuits, however, by an inherent capacity problem: it is increasingly difficult to maintain meaningful relationships as the number of the desired relationships increases. Though a variety of tactics have been implemented to address this problem, most are not fully effective.

A number of exceptional top-performers have found a solution to these challenges through a strategy that provides meaningful differentiation, initiates and maintains positive relationships, and can accommodate large target audiences: awesome client events.

Such events can be effective in promoting a wide variety of client relationships, and incorporating and addressing a wide variety of specific objectives and needs of the organizer.

Though states and qualities of relationships are hard to measure, strong inferences can be drawn from quantifiable aspects of business operations, such as increasing client retention, response and referrals, and initiatives regarding recruiting, human resource development, and team-building.

PART TWO

2

PREFACE

I n Part One, I've attempted to provide a rationale for the inclusion of awesome client events in your practice or business operations. It is meant to answer the question: why would anyone bother? Or, why do many top-performers consider the use of client events to be an important and worthwhile activity?

If I have accomplished my objective, and answered these questions, you may now be wondering *how* you can incorporate this strategy in your own business. Or, if you have already made some attempts in this area, you may be wondering *how* to dramatically improve your results. As well, you may be in a management role, and hoping to provide some instruction, leadership and motivation to others, in the development of their businesses and practices, and wondering *how* to do so.

Part Two addresses those wonderings by identifying and discussing the *four key components* that must be addressed to ensure that objectives are met, and events become awesome. It is about performing the correct steps, efficiently and effectively. It is also about ensuring that client events are not a mere frivolity, but are a highly time-and-cost-effective strategy; so tips on how to avoid common pit-falls and how to reduce costs are included with each *key component*.

"Its like an Italian Wedding," Chef Carlo philosophized proudly—drawing the analogy during one of our interviews, "you've got to figure out who to invite, where the festivities will take place, what the service and reception will be like, how to let everyone know, and how it make it memorable".

Also, like a wedding, the *key components* of a client event, *participants, venue/activity, communications,* and *lasting memories,* should be addressed in the proper order (and are presented as such in this book). To the inexperienced, planning of an event may feel like planning a wedding in that, as the planner becomes immersed in the details, the features of each *component* may prove to be far more complicated than initially expected.

While the intent in Part Two is to offer a "best practices" approach to this subject, I will also attempt to demonstrate the ample opportunity for each business person and professional to infuse there own creativity and personality in the application of this strategy.

FIRST COMPONENT: PARTICIPANTS

Awesome client events, by their very design and purpose, can attract and include a considerable number of participants.

However, those that are new to the strategy, and perhaps participating in, or organizing, their first event, tend to approach the subject of participants cautiously. In my management and consultancy roles, I have experienced several otherwise confident and successful professionals and business owners, "test" this strategy by communicating with only a small number of potential participants.

"I'll start small, and, if I like the results, then the next one will be bigger", they've explained to me.

While I can empathize with their hesitancy, experience in these matters has instilled in me the firm conviction that awesome client events realize their full potential when appropriate levels of effi-ciencies and economies of scale are achieved.

As a rule of thumb, the cost-per-participant-communicated-to tends to decline as the number of participants increases. This re-sults in part from the fact that, while some costs associated with events rise on a per-participant basis, a number of others (such as equipment or room rentals and speaker fees) are fixed costs, re-gardless of the number of participants. This is also due to the fact that some other costs (such as printing or catering) can be reduced on a per-participant basis, when particular minimum thresholds are met. Moreover, and importantly, many participants will never actually attend (which I will clarify), and therefore, cost very little. Finally, some of the largest events—where significant sponsorship, public and media are involved—can actually occur with no cost to the organizer.

Setting aside costs, skittish, would-be event organizers should remember that the primary purpose of the event is to build rela-tionships. As such, the objective is to offer a memorable, bonding, shared experience, for many. It needs to *feel* to the participants like an event (more on this in Second Component: Venue/Activity); the size of the event, and the effort behind it, form an important part of what is being communicated to the participants (more on this in Third Component: Communications).

If you are in a management role, and attempting to introduce a strategy of awesome client events to your (perhaps somewhat skep-tical) team, you may have to lead by example: treating those skeptics as *your* clients, host an event and encourage your team to invite some of their significant, positive relationships. When the power of an awesome event is experienced and shared, your team may be more inclined to follow your lead, host their own event, and confidently approach a growing number of participants.

There is, however, a caveat regarding large events: the organizer must have the skills and resources to diligently follow up with participants. For example, I recall an event that I had organized in Edmonton, Alberta, for my Canadians Retiring Abroad team. In addition to clients and identified prospects, the public was invited to attend. To our delight, approximately 250 guests responded and attended—most of whom were previously unknown to us, and eager to learn more about our services. Unfortunately, our operations were already running at capacity, and we had not prepared a prompt, systematized response. For many of these guests, beyond the event itself, the second impressions of our firm were poor, and many opportunities to provide our services were lost. (This was a mistake that I did not repeat.)

As a culture of relationship-building through client events becomes entrenched in a business or practice, the number of eager participants will grow. I suggest, therefore, that organizers proceed confidently, and trust that, if they follow the suggestions of this book, their events will successfully attract attendees; they should also plan a suitable follow-up in pursuit of the new relationships, and expect that the number and quality of these will increase over time.

Getting Started

When compiling a data base of participants, it might be helpful to consider the following questions:

What is my specific need (beyond general relationship-building)?

Do I have a particular agenda or end-point in mind?

Are you, for example, hoping to grow your business, launch a new product or service to your client or team, retiring, or attempting to achieve some other very specific objective?

Then, given the answer to these questions: what relationships do you need to nurture and/or initiate to accomplish these objectives?

With this effort, it is also important to identify the measurable characteristics that you can monitor. The increase in client retention, or the number of follow-up appointments booked, for example. Naturally, to do this most effectively, it is important to know the current state of those characteristics to which progress can be measured.

Moreover, it is important to be able to attach a value to the achievement of the over-all objective (the implementation of a succession plan, for example) and/or the value associated with the smaller, measurable changes (the average revenue generated by a new client, for example); identifying and quantifying these values, will assist in determining event budgets, and will likely inspire the organizer to larger, and more profitable (on a cost-per-participant) events.

If, for example, a financial advisor knows that a new client generates, on average, $5000 in revenue, and knows that, for every ten couples invited to an event, one new client is referred, then that advisor would likely seek to have as large an event as is practically possible, especially if the cost-per-invited couple declines as the size of the event grows.

Existing Clients

Regardless of the type of business or practice, or any specific pressing agenda it may reflect, a list of participants tends to start with the names of existing clients. What constitutes a *client*, however, will vary. Depending on where the professional, manager and/or business owner is positioned in the distribution chain of a product or service, clients may be end-users, consumers, patients, buyers, distributors, wholesalers, manufacturers, and any combination of these.

While all existing clients may be target participants of an awesome client event, when compiling and updating the data base, many top-performers will give some consideration to the quality of the clients and group them accordingly.

Superior quality clients are typically judged as such based upon factors which include the amount of revenue they currently, directly generate, the amount of revenue they have the potential to generate, and/or the amount of revenue they can indirectly generate (through referrals, influence, contact, association, etc). These are the positive relationships to be maintained: the plates to be kept spinning. Some will conclude that these superior clients should be a higher priority, in terms of event participation, than others.

Moreover, other clients might be considered to be (based upon these criteria) of inferior quality; while it may not mean that they are an inappropriate relationship for the organizer, it may be concluded, though, that they are of relatively low priority as event participants.

This activity of *client segmentation* enhances the organizer's ability to focus their attention and efforts on sub-groups of participants: influenced by the event's specific objectives and agendas, as well as the constraints, such as maximum attendee limits. It also becomes extremely useful when prospect identification, or referral-generating, initiatives are considered.

Identified and Unidentified Prospects

One of the most common uses of client events is to attract and initiate new relationships. Many successful business owners and professionals maintain (either formally or informally) a list of prospective clients, and are in some early stage of relationship development with them. These tend to be co-members of the community or an association, or a friend, relative or associate of a client; as a group, they are known as *identified prospects*.

These participants are to be communicated to directly (through the process as discussed in Third Component: Communications). As with existing clients, identified prospects may undergo a process of segmentation to ensure that the organizer's attentions and efforts are being directed appropriately.

If these non-client participants are wondering why they have been invited to an event that is (predominantly) for clients, try:

"Although you are not yet a client, I think you will really enjoy the event, and it will give me the opportunity to show you how my practice/business is different."

Identified prospects may qualify as such by being a member of an identified group to which the organizer can directly communicate. For example, a professional or business owner that is a member of a local chamber of commerce, rotary club, toastmasters club, etc., may include all the other members as participants in the event's communications effort. Or perhaps the organizer communicates directly to another profession or business. An event-hosting mortgage broker, for example, attempting to attract referrals from realtors, may invite an entire local branch of a real estate firm. I had a most memorable and educational experience directly related to this type of identified prospect relationship-building effort, and gained some insight to some of the interesting challenges that may emerge.

I had been invited to provide a keynote presentation during a luncheon for a group of accountants and lawyers in Kamloops, BC. The organizer was a successful financial planner, and he had identified this group as a potential superior source of client referrals.

After my presentation (on the topic of relationship-building for professionals), the planner made a few remarks, explained a bit about his services, and then boldly addressed the audience. The essence of the interaction went as follows:

"I am regularly referring my clients to lawyers and accountants. But you (as a group) do not seem as ready to refer clients back. Why is that? Is it something to do with my services?"

A lawyer responded (echoing, I believe, the general sentiments of the group) with:

"Our hesitation does not arise from either you or your services. For the sake of our own relationship with the clients, we are generally not comfortable in making referrals regarding their finances".

And then the lawyer added, and this is very important:

*"While we might not provide a referral, we would be happy to provide an introduction...**if the proper social circumstances permitted the opportunity**". (!)*

The planner was able to adapt in light of this insight, and adopt a strategy of awesome client events, with the superior referral sources, and *their* clients, as participants, and with the specific objective of being *introduced* in those social circumstances.

The unidentified prospects are the relationships of those centres-of-influence; they are typically not being communicated to directly, but through the identified intermediary. A second, very significant group of unidentified prospects are the friends, family and associates of clients.

Awesome client events are described as such, in part, because of their ability to inspire clients to provide referrals. Especially after the organizing professional or business owner establishes their reputation with enjoyable and memorable activities, clients will be eager to bring their own guests. These types of clients have been termed "raving fans", and may be motivated by the so-called *law of reciprocity* (tendency to give back), by generously and frequently extolling the virtues and abilities of the event host(s).

The activity of client segmentation may be again useful when considering this group of unidentified prospects. As a rule of thumb, those existing clients that might be deemed superior by virtue of their current and/or future revenue potential tend to associate with other superior prospects (the proverbial *birds of a feather*). Moreover, those existing clients deemed superior by virtue of their ability to refer new superior relationships (those based on revenue potential), need the opportunity to fulfill their propensity. Aided by segmentation, the event organizer can focus efforts and attention suitably on the known intermediaries to access the unknown and unidentified prospects.

Recruiting

If you are manager, partner, broker-owner, or otherwise engaged in some type of human resource initiative, client events can be a very effective relationship-building activity. You may even consider these recruits as your potential clients. As such, many of the principles that apply to other types of clients (segmentation, identified and unidentified prospects, intermediary raving fans, etc) also apply to this group of participants. You may consider addressing your recruit as follows:

"I know you are not a client, but I would like you to attend our event, because I wanted you to experience how we treat our clients. It is this sort of thing that sets us apart in the industry and contributes to our success. This is one of the reasons why people like your self come to our firm/organization and are able to experience their own success."

On the other hand, what makes this group of participants different from other groups is that recruits may also be current or potential competitors. As such, there may be a tendency on the part of the organizer towards secrecy or protectionism regarding the event and their methods. I believe that concerns of this kind are largely without justification, for the following reasons. First, over the long run, people change roles and companies; opportunities for a positive relationship, rather than a competitive relationship, may materialize. Second, as events become larger, and the public and media become participants, it may well become impossible or impractical to screen out competitors from attendance. Third, it has been my experience that most professionals and business owners are not so driven to exceptionality that they are prepared to replicate your efforts; remember, for many, differentiation will not be pursued through their own initiatives regarding purpose, product and process, but by associating themselves with your differentiation. This is not necessarily a short-coming of that person; it is simply pragmatic and expedient. Indeed, it is part of your recruiting pitch to them!

My own recent efforts (toward attracting new positive relationships to Global Exempt Market Solutions) have featured the awesome client event strategy, and recruits have been an important participant. In addition to gaining information regarding our unusual value proposition, they *experience* the process—the event—which would be employed to contribute to their own success, if they were associated with our firm. A snow-ball effect unfolds, as recruits (my new clients) have events for their clients, in which I assist for their benefit, but by which also allows me to attract and include new recruits.

Staff and Stakeholders

Another class of participants is distinguished from those already mentioned by their greater, personal interest in the success of the event, and of your business operations in general. Beyond the participation as an attendee, their role should include responsibilities towards the event's planning and organization. While these efforts are primarily directed towards the advancement of the host's business or practice, they also benefit as stakeholders (positive relationships).

Support staff and assistants, for example, may come to figure prominently as processes become systematized, and a culture of relationship-building through events is established. Top-performers and event enthusiasts report that staff are often keen planners, and come to relish the opportunity to add a new, and potentially very creative and enjoyable, activity to their (often mundane) work load. Awesome client events can be an effective tool for relationship-building among staff, which can produce its own measurable results of retention, response, and referrals. The organizing professional or business owner will need to introduce the concepts and rationale of awesome client events to the team: to foster an understanding how and why the activity is being introduced, and an appreciation of the spirit behind the effort. (To this end, some have provided copies of this book).

There is often, however, an inclination among the team leaders, practice managers, and business owners to full delegation of responsibilities regarding the event. This may not be ideal, as the delegators may miss out on some very rewarding experiences. In my own case, especially as awesome client events began to include travel and exotic destinations, my wife and children became increasingly enthusiastic participants, and some very fond family memories resulted. More positive relationships attended to!

This stake-holder class of participants will include any number of other relationships that will benefit from the event's success: managers, partners of the firm, sales directors, manufacturers, wholesalers, and more. In addition to some planning and promotional support, these parties often have the ability and desire to provide financial assistance. This may be, for example, in the form of full or partial sponsorship (in exchange for recognition, referrals, product placement, etc), or in the form of underwriting the cost of a specific aspect of the event, such as refreshments or gifts (more on this in Fourth Component: Lasting Memories). You may need to entice some of these potential beneficiaries to open up their wallets and purses (and, again, a copy of this book has been known to help).

Event Partners

A particularly effective approach to the organization of an event, especially when it comes to first-time hosts, and smaller practice/business operations, is through the inclusions of *partners.*

These participants tend to have an equal stake in the event's success, and are pursing the advancement of their own business. What was *"your"* event becomes *"our"* event. This class of participants tends to fall into two sub-groups.

One sub-group consists of professionals and business owners that provide different products and services (sometimes to the same client), and perhaps to towards a common objective or in collaboration. For example, a realtor, a mortgage broker, a real estate appraiser, a building inspector, a contractor, a builder and interior designer could unite to create an event. Each could take on a different role in its organization, and each would be responsible for ensuring the participation of their own positive relationships (both in support and as guests). Another example might be a union of an investment advisor, a risk analyst, a lawyer, an accountant and a business appraiser. Inter-business referrals and introductions could be a primary objective of both.

A second sub-group consists of the professionals and other business owners that provide the same services, with whom you associate, and, if there is competition, it is cordial. These may be lawyers or accountants from the same firm, or dentists and related service providers from the same centre, or realtors from the same company, or financial advisors from the same association, and so on.

While many of such groups are self-managing, in other cases there is a partner or director with an interest in the sub-group's success, and whom may be well-inclined to initiate and over-see the planning of the event—with, perhaps, a bit of coaxing.

The attraction of the inclusion of partners as participants arises from the sharing of the work load, the creative synergies, and the economies of scale to be achieved through greater attendance.

Notables and No-shows

Relative to the time expended and the costs incurred to organize the activity, the venue, and the communications strategy for an awesome event, the sending out of a few more invitations is most *in*significant.

As such, I encourage organizers to include many more participants than can and will attend.

As Chef Carlo philosophizes on the spirit of the institution of the Italian Wedding, "To be invited is to be included, so *everyone* is invited!"

His point being that relationship-building occurs from being included in a communications process, even if attendance does not result. So participants can and should include those existing client relationships and identified prospects that reside far from the venue, or are known to be out-of-country on the date of the event, or are unlikely to participate with the proposed travel plans.

Participants can also include well-known figures of your community (such as politicians, professional athletes, media personalities, the president of the local chamber of commerce, etc), or of your company (like a senior vice president, on who's radar screen you would like to show up) even if they have no idea who *you* are. Try communicating to them directly, but keep your own expectations in check; while they may not attend the currently planned event, as your reputation grows, the likelihood that they are able to or inclined to enjoy a future speaker or activity increases.

The attendance of a dignitary or two can be a boon for your business or practice, and of your reputation in the community (and typically at virtually no additional cost). In the days immediately preceding the Bruce Kirkby event, for example, I was so excited about the anticipated attendance levels, that I had already began preparations for the next event. In continuation of the theme of *pursuing adventures*, I had secured the Calgary Zoo and its celebrity-entertainer-educator, Brian Keating. With some additional good luck, Keating was available for, and very interested in, attending Kirkby's presentation. I was able to acknowledge Keating's presence to the rest of the audience and initiate some promotional *buzz* for the next event!

The participation of these *notables* may also provide the organizer with the rare opportunity to network with some extraordinary individuals. A few years ago, I was able to spend time with my favorite Canadian author, and literary hero, Michael Adams. I had been retained to assist a large organization with the planning and managing of an awesome client event in Cancun, Mexico. One of my duties was to arrange for keynote speakers, and so I seized the opportunity to approach Adams, secure his services, and act as his host during his time at the resort. Adams is recognized as one of Canada's most influential intellectuals, and has produced a number award-winning, best-sellers.; two of his books, "Sex in the Snow" and "Better Happy Than Rich", had had a significant impact on my professional work. Getting to know Adams has been one of the high points of my career, and I doubt that this would have occurred were it not for the client event.

The Public

It might not occur to many client event organizers to aspire to draw the attention of the general public. My own initial success in this regard, with Bruce Kirkby, was more by luck than by intent; it was an activity that seemed to take on a life of its own. It gave me the confidence, however, to attempt to replicate, and even improve on, those measurable results on many occasions thereafter.

As one might expect, much larger client/public events tend to result when the activity features someone that is famous. I had been approached by representatives of the Calgary Zoo, for example, to partner on an event that would feature renowned naturalist, Jane Goodall. A venue with the capacity of approximately 2000 was selected (because of the expected interest) and was easily filled: some were my clients as guests, but the majority was the ticket-purchasing public. On another occasion (while researching the first edition of this book), I was invited to participate as a guest and observer in an event featuring Deepak Chopra. For this one, an even larger venue was selected and filled with clients of the event-partners (a successful practice of dentists and some like-minded health care professionals) and, again, with the paying public. For both examples, in affirmation of their special status, the client guests had a different experience (access to the speaker, special seating, and keepsakes) than the paying public. (More on Goodall and Chopra to come)

However, larger client/public events can be produced without the necessity of a famous (and often expensive) anchor or draw. I have organized and participated in a considerable number of events that attracted the interest of the public, to varying degrees, based upon a particularly enticing topic or theme; perhaps the most consistently successful of these was entitled: "Retire to Mexico!" After providing this topic as a key element of an event for my own clients, it was offered to other professionals, and implemented in a number of communities across Western Canada and, to a lesser extent, in Ontario.

While I was generally pleased with turn-outs of approximately 150 in locations like Victoria and Calgary, some others exceeded expectations with the same, or even greater, responses (like 250 in Edmonton, and a delightfully whopping turn-out of 500 in both Saskatoon and Winnipeg). While these participation levels are small relative to those achievable by the likes of Goodall and Chopra, the cost-up-front, effort and, therefore, risks, were less with the smaller events (featuring yours truly).

The participation of the public benefits the organizer by helping to achieve those discussed economies of scale, by attracting a potentially large crowd of unknown and unidentified prospects, and by increasing the perceived significance of the event, and the host's efforts, in the minds of the guests.

Finally, if the public is interested in an awesome event, then it is much more likely that the media will be interested as well, and this can be very significant indeed.

The Media

The relationship between the business owner or professional, the clients, the public and the media can be fascinating and complex. The media is a distributor of information, but it needs its product—its so-called *news*. While it reports what may be of interest to the public, the act of reporting also influences what the public will be interested in. For those that can navigate the complexities, and understand how to *feed* the media, very significant benefits can be realized. So much so, that the "celebrity source" has become an increasingly prevalent phenomenon. These *experts*—representing their industry or profession—are chosen to comment on, or otherwise clarify and add context to, some timely state of affairs: bankers, financial advisors, economists, and health care professionals of various stripes, seem to be the most common. For some of these, like the current president of an organization (the real estate board, the chamber of commerce, etc), the attention is often short-lived; while for others, the status as the go-to source for the local media seems to go on for years. In more recent times, those most successful at cultivating these relationships, and consistently attracting attention, can achieve their own celebrity.

The professional or business owner that can attain this status can enjoy an unusual marketing and branding edge. For existing clients, with the knowledge that their service provider is a media regular, confidence can be instilled, and response and retention is encouraged; for prospects, identified and not, that media presence could factor in the decision to pursue a relationship. Such is the significance of this differentiation that some pursue this media relationship as a separate goal in itself, and consultants, writers and other would-be gurus have been quick to offer guidance.

There is, however, a difficulty in this particular goal. It is an example of an extreme form of competitive goal environment, with few opportunities to pursue, and with very few successful in the pursuit. I believe, therefore, that one cannot merely choose to be a regular media source; there are simply too many factors that are beyond one's control. As well, there are risks associated with publically providing a professional opinion or comment on an important topic; the provider may be erroneous, or misunderstood, or misinterpreted, by the receiving public. For this reason, some organizations, like financial services firms, have been known to adopt and enforce strict rules prohibiting media interaction.

Client events, on the other hand, can be an exceptional lure of media interest, providing it with valuable and timely content for distribution. As the organizer, the host is often an important part of the story, and is the means to access the famous draw speaker, or of more information regarding the enticing topic. Sometimes the reporting occurs in advance of the event, and can promote attendance. This can also reinforce a perception with clients that have already been invited that they will be attending something *newsworthy*. Sometimes the reporting occurs after the event itself and, though not supporting the participation in that particular activity, serves to promote the organizer, and their practice or business, for future relationship-building opportunities. The attractiveness of the story to the media may be enhanced when a community non-profit organization or charity is also a beneficiary of the event (more on this in Second Component). Where the story is about the event, the speaker, the charity, etc., and not about the professional services of the host, (that is, the organizer is not being a media source of comment), making a damaging error in communication is much less of a risk. In other words, the organizing professional or business owner is not attracting the media because of any particular skill they may possess, or fame they may have gained, but because of their association with those so skilled and famed.

Having enjoyed Chef Carlo's years of regular exposure in the newspaper and on television, for his participation in so many newsworthy events, I had been motivated to pursue and cultivate media participation with many of my own activities. As might be expected, I have found that those event features that attract the public (famous speakers, unusual activities, enticing topics), also tend to be of interest to the media, and that attention can become manifest in different ways: newspaper stories before or after the event, requests for written articles regarding the topic, radio interviews, and even appearances on television talk shows, have all resulted from awesome client events.

While the participation of the media, and the public, is not a necessary condition for creating an awesome event, it can be a significant driver of attendance among clients and prospects, and an occasional worthwhile goal for those most desirous of unusual success.

THE BIGGEST, MOST COMMON MISTAKE...

When it comes to the "First Component: Participants", the biggest mistake that is commonly made concerns size; organizers simply think too small. Either through lack of confidence, or lack of imagination, the host attempts to communicate to, and include, too few participants. In these circumstances economies of scale may not be achieved, the small participation may not justify the effort, returns are low, objectives are not met, and the strategy is abandoned. By following the suggestions herein, and adhering to the "Action Steps" below, this mistake can be avoided.

A TIP TO REDUCE COSTS...

Consider including multiple event *partners*. Such an approach will result in a sharing of the organizational responsibilities, and costs; it can also increase the opportunities for sponsorship and other financial support. By increasing the number of hosts, the number of guests should increase, making it more likely to achieve optimal economies of scale, attract members of the public that are willing to pay to attend, and attract the media. When it comes to costs, bigger is almost always much better.

ACTION STEPS...

Prepare a list of all participants. This will include:

Existing clients	segmented and categorized by quality
Identified Prospects	segmented and categorized by quality
Identified Intermediaries	not otherwise listed source of unidentified prospects
Staff	with specific organizational roles
Additional Stakeholders	segmented and categorized by quality
Potential Partners	will include their list of all participants
Notables	a list of high profile individuals that can be communicated to directly
Media	a list a media sources and associated persons that can be communicated to directly

Remember, you will want to include and communicate to more participants than are able to, or inclined to, attend.

The initial efforts towards compiling a list, and segmenting where appropriate, could take some time, but, once completed, will likely require only modest updates for subsequent events.

SECOND COMPONENT: VENUE/ACTIVITY

While the first component (participants) addresses the vast and various potential subjects that the event organizer and host is attempting to reach and touch, the second component addresses the *significance* of that touch.

The venue and the activity are the aspects of the event that make it a memorable, shared, bonding experience. Depending on the specific event, a consideration and selection of one of these elements will necessarily precede the other, and in other cases the two are addressed separately. Sometimes the event planning starts with the venue (a museum, for example) and the activities are dictated or inspired by that decision. In other cases, the event planning starts with the activity (a speaker, for example), and the venue is a secondary consideration. Ultimately, seasoned event planners come to recognize the interdependence of the two aspects, as they contribute to the relationship-building objective of the effort, and tend to consider them simultaneously.

Moreover, this component offers the greatest opportunity for creativity on behalf of the professional, business owner, and their teams; the choices and decisions of venue and activity can reflect the unique personalities of those involved, the culture of their businesses, the brand that they are communicating, and the opportunities available in their community.

Despite the potential for creative and personalized expression, I believe that particular venue/activity combinations are qualitatively different from others, as they serve the relationship-building objective. With this in mind, I strongly recommend that event organizers adhere to the following principle: the event should feature a venue/activity combination that the guests could not easily organize or just choose to do on their own.

For example, simply providing participants with tickets for a concert, theatrical production, or sporting event, that is readily available to the public (and is quite possibly the kind of thing they have done on many previous occasions), by itself, is not likely to result in an awesome event; making an impression on the participants will require a more significant touch.

Traditional Venues

When selecting the location for an awesome client event, it is helpful to think of those venues as falling into two primary categories; the first, and most obvious of these, I refer to as *traditional venues.*

These types of locations are those specifically designed to accommodate a large number of participants, and were likely built specifically for the purpose of hosting a gathering. Traditional venues are facilities like theatres, hotel ballrooms, convention/meeting centres, and sporting arenas. They are the kinds of locations that we are all familiar with, have been to on many occasions, and are, likely, the first locations we think of when contemplating an event. Other than the specific activity therein, though, it is rare that these types of venues are an attraction in themselves.

The suitability of, and, thus, popularity of, traditional venues is derived from their convenience, accessibility and familiarity. They tend to be centrally located, with ample parking and restrooms in abundance; they are readily available, and provide all the technological and gastronomic services that we may require. Clients know where to go and where to park. They are an easy choice.

However, those attractions are also the repulsions; traditional venues are often too familiar, too obvious. Clients have been to these with sufficient regularity, that there maybe nothing particularly memorable about that aspect of the event. Without sufficient venue significance, the touch of the event may quickly fade away.

Ironically, though often an inferior selection for events, traditional venues are often the more expensive selection. Since the purpose of the venue is to accommodate crowds and events, that is also their revenue opportunity. In addition to the price of the room itself, incidentals, such as screens, microphones, projectors, and, especially refreshments, are usually ala carte, and the costs can add up quickly.

Despite their short-comings, some traditional venues, like a prominent, landmark hotel, can be an ideal location for an event, especially where it helps to set a superior ambience or mood, or it distinctly reflects the brand, character and/or culture of the business or practice. Traditional venues can also be the best option when the host community offers few choices, or for events that are particularly large. In such circumstances, however, efforts should be made to customize or personalize the experience of key participants if possible.

Both the Goodall and Chopra events, for example, occurred at a traditional venue (Calgary's Jubilee Theatre and Telus Convention Centre respectively)—a decision that was dictated primarily by the need to accommodate the expectedly large audience. However, to ensure that the clients were able to enjoy an enhanced experience, an exclusive seating area and a private reception was organized for those guests with the headlining personalities.

Nontraditional Venues

I refer to the second category of potential event locations as nontraditional venues. These are the venues that were not, perhaps, specifically designed to host gatherings, and typically, do not readily come to mind when we think of events. Historically, those managing the nontraditional venues may not even have considered their facilities as ideal for events; that realization may have been an afterthought, or may represent the *evolution* of the venue in response to market demand, and/or the need for additional sources of revenue.

The category of nontraditional venues tends to be comprised of museums, art galleries, zoos, planetarium/science exhibits, historically significant locations, specialty parks, etc. Some of these venues are quite unusual. I had been invited to attend an event that took place at the top of the ski jump that had been created for Calgary's 1988 Winter Olympics. The tower stands prominently on a ridge near the west end of the city and features a breath-taking panoramic view of the Bow River Valley and Rocky Mountains. The only reason I attended that event was because I had been driving past the tower for several years, and had always wondered what that view would be like; now, when I drive past, I am always reminded of that event. On another occasion, I had been asked to speak at a client event in Winnipeg which took place at the Canadian Mint (an appropriate venue, as my presentation was about money management and investments).

Sourcing and securing an unusual venue can be a bit more of an effort for the organizer. Some imagination may be required. Also, the host may face more responsibility with preparations, perhaps needing to arrange for, setting up, and taking down, chairs, tables, projection screens, signs, decorations, food and refreshments, etc. Also, since such venues may not have been designed with these specific purposes in mind, one may have to contend with and work around issues regarding visibility and acoustics. As guests may not be fully familiar with the nontraditional venue, the host may also need to provide guests with additional information: directions to the location, parking instructions, clothing requirements, the impact of adverse weather conditions, and the like. This requirement becomes particularly relevant when it comes to client events that involve travelling.

With this extra effort and responsibility, however, the organizer is likely to experience a (sometimes dramatically) reduced cost. This is especially the case when it comes to catering services. Almost all traditional venues, and some nontraditional venues, require the use of their own, in-house catering services—which can add significantly to the budgetary requirements. Nontraditional venues are the most likely opportunities for the organizer to address this issue by using their own resources for food and drink.

Beyond potential-cost savings, the most important benefit of a nontraditional venue is its significance of impact on the participants. These locations are often a destination or draw in themselves. They are the kinds of public/private spaces that attract our clients and prospects, even when there is no special activity taking place. As such, that can be a most memorable feature of the event, and contribute to long-term relationship building. Ideally, when a participant thinks of that venue in the future—when they drive by it, or the venue is in the news—they are reminded of the host and the experience they had together.

Passive Elements

In conjunction with venue, the second factor that contributes most notably to the significance of the event is the activity or activities that will be taking place. For these, there are predominantly two features or characteristics to consider: the *passive elements* and the *interactive elements.*

Passive elements are those event conditions that establish the guests as an audience. Typically, these activities would include theatrical performances, sporting events, and keynote speakers. These are also the sorts of event activities that would be most closely associated with traditional venues. As such, when events are primarily passive in nature, there is often the opportunity to accommodate larger audiences, and with less of an effort.

However, with such passive events, there is a risk that the organizer will simply rely on those sporting and theatrical activities that have already been organized, and to which the participants could attend on their own. The ramifications of a host taking this relatively easy approach is that, if participants have already had many very similar experiences, there may be nothing significant about the one associated with the proposed event. As indicated above, the guiding principle for the venue/activity combination is to offer something that the guests could not easily choose to do or organize on their own.

With this principle in mind, many top-performing professionals and business owners that adopt the awesome client event strategy will arrange for interesting, exciting and memorable keynote speakers as the passive element of their planned activity. When selecting a speaker, some might be initially inclined to consider a speaker whose topic is closely associated with the professional services or products of the organizer. This can be a critical error, as what might be of interest to the host, may not really be of any particular interest to the audience—at least not enough to entice them to attend; participants may feel, for example, that they are being drawn into a sales process, rather than being provided with a relationship-building opportunity. Moreover, organizers are likely to discover that the featuring of such speakers and topics will severely limit the attractiveness of the event for some participants, such as potential event partners and stake-holder sponsors.

Speakers whose topic's feature generally interesting themes, or include inspiring stories of struggles and accomplishment, or of the wonder of nature, can offer a broad appeal to a diverse range of participants. Indeed, the best of these—the so-called *professional* speakers—are often cleverly adept at combining an array of such topics, themes and issues into a very memorable experience. For example, through the stories of Bruce Kirkby, Jane Goodall, Brian Keating, and Dave Rodney, my clients and I have *"explored"* the jungles of Africa, the inhospitable expanses of the Arabian Desert, the wilds of the Serengeti, and the extreme dangers at the summit of Mt Everest.

In addition to such escapism and story-telling, appropriate speakers may include those that specialize in more practical, pressing or serious topics. These might include: health and longevity, futurism and technology, or conservationism and environmentalism. Care should be taken, however, by the organizer to ensure that the specific message is appropriate and comfortable for the audience.

In more recent years, I have carefully sought to bring these sorts of *adventure* subject areas closer to my professional activities by providing (what I call) *cross-over* presentations. One of the more popular of these keynote presentations, for example, is titled *"Adventures in Retirement".* In this presentation, I have covered topics such as issues related to demographics and the changing concepts of "retirement" and "leisure", with stories of how baby boomers are enabled to pursue their own adventures. A second, typically longer cross-over presentation is entitled *"Retire to Mexico!"*: which covered such topics as how, where, and why baby boomers are enjoying an exciting, snow-bird or expatriate retirement lifestyle, in Mexico (and other exotic destinations). In these and other cross-over presentations the objective was to inform, entertain and inspire the participants—many of whom were no longer likely to attempt their own Mt Everest summit.

Interactive Elements

The second characteristic concerning the event activity to be considered are the *interactive elements;* these are the features which encourage the participants to become physically and verbally engaged at the venue.

Interactive elements are extremely important in support of the primary objectives of memorable, shared experiences and relationship-building. It is a recognized strategy in education, for example, that a student may be better able absorb, recall and apply ideas, information and experience when interactivity is featured (as apposed to merely being lectured to); that is to say, an event can produce a more significant touch when the participants are invited to do something.

Interactive elements are often associated with nontraditional venues, and may require that specific venue for the desired engagement. For example, an event at a museum may include a guided tour with a curator, or an event at a winery may include a tour and tasting, or an event at a restaurant may include an opportunity to prepare (and then enjoy) a delicacy.

In Calgary's inner city up-and-coming community of Bridgeland is an unusual, innovative and popular restaurant, *The Main Dish*. The food preparation occurs within (what can best be described as) a "multiple open-kitchen" concept, and includes a separate wine bar and desert station. Though in-door, out-door, and cocktail style seating is available, very often customers are walking around, mingling with staff, and talking to the chefs—while they are preparing the food! To round off the experience, there is often live music and impromptu cooking demonstrations. Essentially, one feels as if they are a guest at the owner's home, and the party is in the kitchen. The Main Dish represents an evolution of the restaurant experience from passive to highly interactive, and, as a result, has become a great venue for business meetings and client events.

Popular leisure pursuits can be a great inspiration for interactive elements, and also allow for some flexibility and creativity with venue selection. For example, an interest in golf, may lead to a group golf lesson with a pro, and an afternoon on a putting green; or an interest in reading, may lead to a writers workshop with a well-known scribe, at a trendy bookstore; or an interest in home decorating, may lead to a feng shui presentation, at a Buddhist temple.

As I have spent much of the last ten years providing professional development training and consulting on the topics of awesome client events, I am often approached by event enthusiasts that are proud to share their own creative approaches to interactivity. One particularly clever example was described to me by a manager in the financial services industry. The event took place in the Greater Vancouver area, at a garden centre, and featured (appropriately for the region) a presentation on gardening. The participants were engaged with their pots and plants, as well as each other, while the garden centre was happy to have the opportunity to promote its products and services, and the organizer was providing a memorable experience.

Unlike venue/activity combinations that feature passive elements, those that feature interactive elements tend to suffer from constraints on the size of the event and the number of guests, as well as added organization responsibilities. However, the interactive element of an event not only affords the guest with the opportunity to learn and grow by doing, but it allows for that experience to occur alongside the host and other guests. This could be the most prominent relationship-building catalyst of any of the components, features and elements associated with awesome events.

Food and Refreshments

The inclusion of eating and drinking as an interactive element of an event—especially when it comes to alcohol—can be problematic, costly and is, therefore, hotly debated. The choices concerning this topic will reflect a wide range of factors including: budget, the specific disposition of the stake-holder and partner participants, the attending guests, the venue/activity combination of the event, and the culture and personality of the hosting professional, business person, and their team.

Clearly, there will be instances where food and/or drink figure prominently in the event (wine-tasting, cooking demonstrations, etc). And yet, some have attempted to offer those refreshments as more like bait or a bribe, rather than an enticing and creative component of an awesome event. Having organized and participated in events with a wide range of approaches to the issue of food, I have adopted the following rules of thumb.

First, where the events are small, and participating guests are few, and the relationships are already significant (high quality clients, and significant partners and stakeholders), a dinner or lunch, and, at times, including alcohol, is more likely to be appropriate. With my recent efforts for Global Exempt Market Solutions, we have adopted this model, and distinguish it from other similar activities with the title: *focus group*. Though these lack the economies of scale associated with larger client event formats, the return on the effort, given the quality of the participants, can be significant.

Second, the inclusion of meals and beverages are most appropriate when the participating guests are fully expecting to, and happy to, pay for those themselves. There tends to be three types of circumstances where this will take place: events that include a charitable or fund-raising component and the guests are buying tickets; events that include an opportunity for a select group of guests to spend time with the famous draw entertainer or speaker, at a cost to those guests; travel events, and the clients are covering the entire cost (more on this later).

Third, as the number of participating guests increases, the likelihood that full meals and refreshments should be provided (at no cost to the guest) and their prominence at the event decreases.

I have been most fortunate in my event planning efforts to have had access to some very capable and experienced resources. One of those I have consulted with regularly, especially on the topic of food and refreshments, is my brother-in-law, Chef Carlo. He is an advocate of a four step process:

Step#1 Select a Professional

Just as you would want your clients to rely on your professional expertise, place your trust and confidence in a professional caterer. The best of these are also successful business owners and entrepreneurs, with valuable insight and resources. Seek out their services through referral and reputation, and build a positive relationship with familiarity and accountability; they can become stake-holders in your success as well. When seeking their guidance, be clear and articulate with your specific objectives (client retention, client referral, client response, recruiting, team-building, succession planning, etc).

Step#2 Select a Style of Food

The types of food and refreshments provided should reflect the purpose of the event. If guests are to remain seated, a hot and heavy meal might help. Unless the event is specifically celebratory, the serving of alcohol should occur in moderation, or not at all. Events that are designed to promote interaction and mingling would be best accompanied by light snacks and finger food. If a particular theme has been selected, or is dictated by the venue/activity combination, let the caterer help you find that fine line between to much and too little theme detail. When a full meal is being provided, and is a featured activity of the event, request a "test" meal from the caterer.

Step#3 Select a Style of Service

As with the style of food, the style of service should reflect the purpose of the event. If the mood is meant to be serious and formal, then seated clients, with full service to the table, might be the best choice. This option, however, requires more time and is often more expensive than other styles. A variation of the full service style, which is less formal and less expensive, is known as farm style: waiters deliver large platters to the table and guests serve themselves. The buffet style works well when time is more limited, when the setting is less formal, and where a budget is limited. Butler style service has the staff wondering among the guests with trays of finger foods and, perhaps, champagne; this style works well when guest mingling is being encouraged. The style of service selected may be influenced considerably by the choice of the venue; some nontraditional venues, in particular, because of the layout or shape of the room, or the physical interaction and engagement that may take place, will limit the viability of service styles.

Step#4 Prepare a Contingency Plan

Every seasoned caterer can recall an event or two that did not go exactly to plan. The hosts tend to imagine the activities unfolding with only the best case scenarios in mind, but unforeseen circumstances, such as inclement weather, traffic jams, difficulties arising at the venue, issues with delivery of food and beverages, etc., can (and will) arise. Organizers should imagine worst case scenarios and prepare a contingency action plan.

Combining the Elements

As the planning of an awesome client event unfolds, organizers should recognize and consider how these various elements (traditional and nontraditional venues, passivity and interactivity, food and drink) will contribute to the success of the event. Often, it is a creative combination of these features that distinguishes excellent and memorable relationship-building activities from others that are less impactful. With some experimentation and practice, the elements can be brought together such that the strengths of each (rather than their shortcomings), serve to enhance their guests' experience. Here are a few examples.

One of my very favorite client events became known affectionately as the African Safari Adventure. The primary draw and attraction for this event was a well-known television and radio personality, author and naturalist, Brian Keating. He would provide a highly entertaining presentation featuring his recent tour of Africa, with music and video. The venue selected was a private reception and education facility at the Calgary Zoo (ranked as one of North America's best). Before and after the presentation, non-alcohol refreshments were served, and guests could interact with the docents (zoo volunteers) and the guest-friendly animals (snakes, birds, etc) brought out specifically for the event, as well as with a special guest (from a previous event): Bruce Kirkby. Guests were also provided with an exclusive introduction to the Calgary Zoo's plans for its significant redevelopment. (This redeveloped area would become the venue for a future event as well).

During Keating's presentation, guests were a passive audience; before and after, guests were highly verbally and physically engaged with docents, animals, and each other. The venue—the zoo—provides the benefits of a traditional venue (location, accessibility, familiarity, resources, support), but it also provided an exclusive room, and unusual access for guests to docents, animals, and expansion plans, all with a decidedly nontraditional ambience. The refreshments were only a secondary feature of the activity, but, as expected, promoted a lively comingling of participants (that Kirkby would later describe as feeling like a "reunion of friends"). It was an event that they could not easily organize on their own, or just choose to do.

A more recent event was inspired, not by a personality or speaker, but by the venue: The Cantos Music Foundation. Cantos is an extraordinary museum of piano (and piano-like) musical instruments, and has been referred to as Calgary's best-kept secret. A private and highly interactive guided tour was provided to all guests (in groups of approximately 20 at a time). As the museum access was exclusively for the event, part of its facilities had been organized as a reception lounge, with finger food and a wine bar, where guests mingled before and after their turn to explore the exhibits. I also provided a short presentation (mostly an expression of thanks and appreciation), and an acknowledgement of the event sponsor (who had set up an information/promotion booth). The shape and size of the venue, and the nature of the activity, limited the number of participants, so the same event was repeated for an additional group the following night.

The participants enjoyed a predominantly interactive experience, and were passive only briefly—during my address. The venue was predominantly nontraditional, and, indeed, largely unknown to the guests, but was traditional enough to be centrally located, and provide the resources required for a successful event. In particular, as a private foundation and facility, I was able to arrange for the food and wine myself, at a fraction of the cost that I would have endured at a traditional venue. The inclusion of wine, and a back-drop of gentle piano music, helped to establish a relaxed mood and a refined tone, inviting the guests to linger.

In striking contrast to the Cantos event, I can also recall the most outrageous and lively activity I have organized: The Pirate Ship Adventure!

I had been retained by a large and prominent investment manufacturer to organize a conference for their most significant clients:

approximately 70 of their top financial advisors. The primary venue selected was an award-winning, truly exceptional, all-inclusive resort just south of Cancun, Mexico. While much of the conference featuring professional development and educational programs, as well as "free time" for unstructured relationship-building, exploring and recharging, I was also intent on organizing a single, enjoyable, memorable activity for the entire group. For several reasons, this proved to be a surprisingly difficult task.

First, in addition to those 70 target relationships, their spouses and travel partners were also in attendance, as well as the host's staff, bringing the total to approximately 150 participants—a potential logistical challenge in a foreign country. Second, in that I was only moderately familiar with the area and its amenities, keeping true to my interest in effectively combining elements of passivity, interactivity, venue, and food and drink, might prove to be impossible. Third, in that the target participants were all successful, worldly, well-travelled, out-going, high-income earners, I was very concerned as to whether or not I had the ability and imagination to arrange something truly unusual and memorable. Could I adhere to my own guiding principle: arrange an activity that they could not easily organize, or simply decide to do, on their own?

With some diligent research, and help from my lovely wife (an expert travel partner), we found the solution to this challenge on a pirate ship. We arranged to have the guests picked up at the resort by four buses, and delivered to a pier in central Cancun, where they boarded a replica pirate ship complete with very enthusiastic Mexican pirates (and were joined in spirit by some of the guests who had brought their own surprising realistic pirate outfits!). As the sun set and the ship sailed off into the bay, guests were treated to a buffet dinner, lots of drinks, and a very funny and lively audience participation show. The performance concluded with a hostile exchange of cannon fire with another pirate ship (and its own guests enjoying the same experience), and sword fighters boarding each others' vessel—to everyone's roars of encouragement. Successful in our "battle", the ship was converted to a floating disco for hours of celebratory dancing! Even for the most travelled of guests, the night's activity proved to be highly memorable and enjoyable.

Sourcing the Next Opportunity

In most communities, where most professionals and business owners operate, and in which most of our current and future relationships reside, there are any number of interesting venues available for relationship-building experiences to occur. Having learned about a few of the events that I have organized, you might already be coming up with a list of suitable venue/activity combinations for yourself.

As well, you may discover that, as a culture of awesome client event planning grows within your business or practice, members of your team, your associates and event partners, and even your clients, will become more aware of those opportunities. This developing skill will be important as you proceed, for, over time, it will take more creativity and imagination to source new and novel selections to draw and entertain your positive relationships. Moreover, as you experience success, your competitive nature may drive you to maintain, or improve upon, the standards you set, and the expectations of your clients.

With this in mind, event organizers would be wise to consider not only the current venue/activity opportunities, but the future ones as well. Providing the means for participants to be among the *first* to experience a high-profile venue in your community, for example, can be an effective enticement for attendance and a significant contributing factor to a successful event. I decided to conduct some research, specifically for this book, with the objective of finding the most attractive emerging venue/activity opportunities within a half hour *walk* from my office. Here is what I learned.

The Cantos National Music Centre

This facility is expected to be like nothing else in Canada: a museum, recording studio, and live music venue where music is created, performed, recorded, discussed and celebrated. The Centre will be the entrance to Calgary's highly anticipated inner-city redevelopment, the East Village, and pre-designs suggest an attractive mix of modern architecture and restored heritage buildings. A focal point of the project will be the renovation of the King Edward Hotel, a landmark blues-bar-hotel affectionately known as the King Eddy, which is hoped to be completed in time for the 100th anniversary celebration of the Calgary Stampede in 2012. With an anticipated price tag of approximately $120 million, the venue will likely attract considerable media attention, and generate a substantial buzz throughout Calgary, and beyond.

The Bow

Calgary's most obvious construction project is the crescent-shaped skyscraper slowly emerging from the city's downtown core, a few blocks from its namesake, the Bow River. Upon completion, it will be the tallest building in Canada (outside of Toronto), with the third largest foundation in the world (after Howard Hughes Center, LA, and Sama Tower, Dubai). At an estimated cost of $1.4 billion, the tower will change Calgary's skyline and provide truly spectacular views. Though primarily an office complex, rumours suggest that tour guides will be required, and the plans also provide for three sky gardens—which may provide unique client event venue opportunities. From traffic flow disruptions and construction drama, to issues regarding its financing and costs, the media has and will continue to enjoy ample newsworthy material, and the public will be increasingly curious to experience The Bow upon completion.

Telus World of Science

Calgary's science centre is getting ready to move to a brand new, $160 million, world class venue. The landmark building is part of a high-profile redevelopment, along major transportation routes, and is adjacent to the Calgary Zoo. Billed as a celebration of science, technology and art, the facility proposes to engage and inspire its guests, and to cultivate curiosity, exploration and discovery. Combining 5 main galleries, an atrium, and a theatre, the centre has been designed specifically with events in mind; resources and support services will be available for organizers, and the venue is expected to accommodate up to 500 guests. The buzz around this venue is sure to grow in anticipation of its planned opening (late 2011), and will certainly become a favored choice for awesome client events.

Each of these future venue opportunities, though different in important respects, shares some of the same characteristics that make them worthy of consideration. They are interesting and exciting additions to the community (non-traditional venues), but are centrally located and will provide the necessary resources for an event (traditional). They each have the potential to provide some form of unusual, engaging and memorable activity, with both passive and interactive elements. Finally, with the increasing profile of these venues in the community, guests, sponsors, partners, etc, will be easily enticed, and eager to participate. Within a half hour walk from my office, not only did I very quickly discover these three excellent opportunities for event venues and activities, but I felt that sense of excitement about the prospect of treating some of my positive relationships to an unusual and memorable experience.

Moreover, it seems that there is a trend among the creators of these facilities, whether very large or very small, to consider how they will give value to a guest, a host or an event organizer. The venues are designed with client event planning as an objective: with services and support conceptualized at the out-set. It is as if in recognition of the need to adapt and differentiate, as a destination, in a highly competitive environment. If so, those professionals and business owners looking to differentiate themselves (with relationship-building events) should take some comfort in the fact that resources and solutions are very likely available—and new one's emerging—in their own community.

THE BIGGEST, MOST COMMON MISTAKE...

When it comes to the "Second Component: Venue/Activity", the biggest mistake that is commonly made is that the event planner thinks that there is something so inherently interesting about what they do for a living that they are determined to turn some feature of their business into an activity. This mistake is typically manifest in a presentation topic and speaker closely associated with the host's profession or business. The organizer should consider that a great many client relationships form because of products and services that are not, in and of themselves, desired by the clients; rather, they are a means (or even a necessary evil) to some truly desirable end: health, autonomy, fulfilling relationships, personal growth and development, memorable life experiences, etc. Venue and activities that support the pursuit and achievement of these more desirable objectives are far more likely to be awesome.

A TIP TO REDUCE COSTS...

Well-chosen nontraditional venues can provide the host with the best of both worlds: interesting, memorable and fun locations, for often a fraction of the cost of traditional venues. With some imagination, creativity and experience, event organizers can arrange for venues that include activities, and allow the opportunity for the host to provide their own beverages and food. Where these venues are novel or completely new to the guests, further differentiation is established, and the significance of the touch is enhanced.

ACTION STEPS

On going…

Prepare a list of potential traditional venues

Prepare a list of nontraditional venues

Prepare a list of potential activities featuring passive elements

Prepare a list of potential activities featuring interactive elements

Update list with future potential venues and activities

To be completed 6 months to one year before the event…

Select the activity, confirm availability, and secure

Select the venue, confirm availability, and secure

Determine venue capacity relative to desired attendance; adjust either if required

Approximately one month before the event…

Determine food and refreshment needs, follow Chef Carlo's four steps

Confirm and organize requirements for activity (speaker's needs, for example)

One week before the event…

Visit venue, review/rehearse event, confirm sundry requirements (signage, tables, chairs, decorations, microphone, projector, etc)

THIRD COMPONENT: COMMUNICATIONS

T he venue/activity combination can be thought of as a product, with a very particular target market in mind—the participants. As such, the host will need an effective marketing strategy to bring the two together. This is the important role of the third component, communications.

As with other marketing strategies, the primary purpose of the communications program is to increase the likelihood that the target market takes the action desired by the communicator: attendance at the event. Marketing experts report that a target market may require several communiqués before the desired activity occurs, and that the likelihood of such activity may increase proportionately with quality and quantity of the communication pieces. With this in mind, successful event organizers tend to adopt a marketing strategy with several steps.

There is often a secondary purpose to the communications effort; generally, these may be more about branding, or reaffirming established consumer—vendor relationships, than about prompting a sale or transaction. When it comes to the communications regarding awesome client events, however, the secondary purpose is to foster relationship development, even when attendance does not occur. As such, the design and implementation of the communications strategy should reflect this purpose.

Where the communications program is successful in its primary purpose, and attendance in generated, the event host is then provided with an often-rare opportunity to communicate directly to a group representing a cross-section of, perhaps, their most significant positive relationships. Therefore, the organizer should prepare to capitalize on those relationship-building moments with a well-crafted and sincere message.

The Medium is Part of the Message

When considering these purposes, and opportunities, and the many steps that might constitute a fully-formed communications campaign, some event planners may become overwhelmed by the details to be attended to, and the magnitude of the effort. They may tell themselves that the venue and activity are sufficiently enticing, and the guest list is sufficiently long, that a simple invitation will suffice in generating the desired action. First reluctant and complacent, the organizer then becomes surprised and disappointed when the event is poorly attended.

In other cases, the host may approach this component with the some of the dispositions that have supported them in their efforts to be successful business owners and professionals; they might seek to be efficient, for example, by combining steps in the communications process, or by delegating away their opportunities to participate to staff, associates, event partners, etc. Then they are disappointed when the event is well-attended, but the measurable indicators of relationship-building (retention, referral, response, recruiting, etc) do not meet expectations.

To avoid these potential pit-falls, organizers should approach the communications component with the following philosophy: the medium is the message. That is to say, the event itself is a form of communication. The fact that you have taken the time, directed the energy and resources, with the best of intentions, to provide a memorable experience, is saying something to the guests (and even to those no-shows). It is the effort itself that leads to the results of enhanced relationships. As such, for the event to be a fully effective medium, the efforts behind the organization of the participants, the venue, and the activity must be matched with a comparable effort behind the communications strategy. That effort should be obvious to the participants.

By making a full effort with communications, the participants are being touched, and with some significance; by actively participating in that process, the host is affirming *their* interest and intent regarding the relationship.

Moreover, the significance of an event experience often rises in cor-relation to the number of participating guests. For larger events, full, maximum capacity attendance should be the objective, not only for the economies of scale, but because, no matter how many people are at a venue, a half-full room still looks, feels and sounds like a half-full room to the guests. Remember, the event should *feel* like an event.

To accomplish these attendance and client touch objectives, with an obvious effort, I and my team tend to implement a program of communications featuring four steps prior to the event, and one step during.

Step #1: The Buzz

Long before an event actually takes place, while the many organiza-tional details are being identified and addressed, the hosts will find a growing, almost tangible, mood of enthusiasm. This energy can be shared with all the participants, and it can serve a very practical purpose.

The target market of your communications strategy is already over-loaded with information. They are the recipient of countless of pieces of news and advertisements every day: television, radio, print ads, billboards, traditional print mail, e-mail, on-line adver-tisements, text messages, phone, and more. While some of this in-formation will be useful to, welcomed and desired by, the audience, a great deal of it is classified as useless intrusions, distractions, junk and spam. Unfortunately, and very importantly, the audience will often lose sight of the necessary and desirable communications in the deluge of the undesirable ones. This is especially likely if the target audience is unaware that a welcomed communication piece is coming.

The buzz refers to those, often unstructured, elements of a communications program that lets the target audience—the participants—know that something interesting, and even exciting, is being prepared specifically for them. The buzz is to ensure that the guests are aware of, and expecting, a formal communication: an invitation. If the invitation is unexpected, it is much more likely to be missed in the avalanche of junk information.

The purpose of Step #1, The Buzz	**To put participants in a state of *anticipation* for Step #2.**

While much of the buzz will happen naturally and automatically, especially if some new and exciting venue/activity has been selected, organizers can also implement an effort to encourage that sense of awareness and anticipation. When I first began to adopt a strategy of awesome client events, I had a fairly structured financial planning practice, with a set schedule of face-to-face appointments to review the progress of the plan. I made a habit of ending the meetings with a comment about the up-coming event:

"Oh, and by the way, you may want to circle April the 6th on your calendar; we have organized another very special event, and I am sure you are going to have fun; it's a bit of a surprise still, but watch out for those invitations; they are being sent out in March".

As my business grew, and the number of relationships that I was managing exceeded capacity, the processes become more systematized; these came to include the sending of a year-end letter that featured a schedule of activities for the up-coming year, indicating: months dedicated to client review appointments, the topics to be addressed, months dedicated to new client acquisition, weeks for professional development, my holiday/travel schedule, and the date of the next awesome client event. The purpose of the schedule was not only to set clients expectations appropriately, but to contribute to the anticipation buzz of the event planning and communications process.

Professionals and business owners whose operations include a fixed physical work environment that is frequented by clients and other positive relationships enjoy additional opportunities to establish that buzz with well-placed teaser communication pieces like posters and announcements. (Much more on this in Fourth Component: Lasting Memories). As a culture of event planning is established in that business, and clients become (albeit, perhaps, unconsciously) aware of its contribution to the brand, it becomes easier for the organizers to build the buzz, until, eventually, participants are in anticipation of being in anticipation. That is, they are aware that special activities are in the works, always, because the host is just that sort of top-performer.

The creation of the buzz works exceptionally well when, at one event, one can already begin to create a buzz about the next event, or an up-coming travel activity. Having Brian Keating stand and be recognized as a special guest at the Bruce Kirkby event, for example, also gave me the opportunity to start a buzz regarding the next event, featuring Keating. Providing the opportunity for guests at the first Calgary Zoo event to preview the massive zoo expansion, the Destination Africa exhibits and facilities, gave me the opportunity to build a buzz for future events that occurred at that soon-to-be-created venue. Many of the Retire to Mexico presentations also included some promotion regarding the upcoming related travel activities. While, more recently, the Cantos Music Foundation event has helped to establish a buzz around the highly anticipated relocation and grand re-opening of the new facilities, which will very likely be a venue for a future event.

The buzz can be used to create anticipation among the target market, but it can also position the idea of an event among future participants. For example, any number of associates, stake holders and potential event partners may become aware that something exciting is going on, and they are *not* included, or not included to the extent that they might like to be. When they are approached to participate (perhaps as a sponsor or organizing partner) in a future event, they will already be well-aware of the host's success, experience and reputation in this regard, and, as such, may be far more inclined to participate.

Step #2: The Invitation

With the target market in anticipation of more information, a formal communication piece is required. This piece, the invitation, is meant to accomplish a few important tasks. First, it must arouse interest in the participant by simply stating the draw or attraction—the venue/activity combination. For example:

"You are invited to an evening with Jane Goodall, at the Jubilee Theatre, with a very special, private reception to follow!"

Creating that statement can provide some insight for the organizer as to the possible success of that event. For example, does it sound like and feel like an event? Does it truly seem appropriate to end the statement with an exclamation mark?

The invitation must also provide a couple of key pieces of information to the recipient: the date, the time, for example. However, a common mistake among event planners is to ask too much of the invitation: to over communicate at that single step in the communication processes. It is *not* the purpose of the invitation to tell the participant every detail.

The purpose of Step #2, The Invitation	To incite the recipients to act—to RSVP, Step #3.

Rather than provide all those details up front, the invitee is now obliged to provide a reciprocal effort; the invitation must instruct them to respond:

"Please RSVP for tickets and more information".

In addition to the fairly minimal amount of actual information expressed with the invitation, it communicates effectively by its form and delivery. For example, the graphic design of the invitation should be thoughtful, and reflect, perhaps, the theme or location of the event. Thankfully, the proliferation of design software seems to have enhanced the readily available and skilled services, and reduced their cost. As with other event stake-holders, I have, over time, sought to build-relationships with such creative graphic artists, printers, and other resources to ensure attractive, timely and cost-effective work support. However, there also seems to be an emerging trend among venue and activity providers to have pre-created, "sample" communications pieces available as an added value of their services to the event organizers: perhaps generally increasing the quality, while reducing the associated effort and costs.

One common cost-saving measure that *should not* be pursued is in regards to the delivery of the invitation. Despite the obvious popularity of electronic communications, I very strongly believe that invitations should exist in three-dimensions, be mailed or hand-delivered, and be attractive enough to get posted on the fridge! While three dimensional communications are more likely to result in an RSVP response than their two dimension counterparts, they are also much more likely to be kept (more on this in Fourth Component: Lasting Memories). Unlike those communications pieces that merely arrive electronically, those on the fridge also communicate to others: those unidentified prospects and potential new relationships. As well, the experience of such printed and mailed invitations can be further enhanced with matching, designed envelopes, and sealed by, or otherwise decorated with, stickers, etc. Remember, the medium—the effort—is an important part of the message.

As discussed regarding the first component (participants), having already undertaken the effort and costs associated with arranging the venue and activity, and designing and creating the invitations, event organizers should be most generous with their communications effort; many more participants can and should be communicated to than will attend, and that the venue can accommodate. Therefore, invitations should be sent to all of (or the appropriate sub-group of) that long list of potential guests (as tallied at that first action step), and the delicate balance of ensuring full attendance versus turning away disappointed participants is pursued.

Since additional communication steps follow the invitation, it should be received by the participants at least a month in advance, and the organizer should be prepared for the RSVP process to follow. If the media is included on the participation list, this advanced notice may be of particular importance as it will allow interested parties enough time to consider whether or not the event will be of interest to the public—whether or not it is newsworthy. The media may require more information about the venue and activity, as well as the event's purpose, than will be communicated on the invitation alone.

Step #3: The RSVP

The RSVP is an interactive process, and detailed record keeping will likely be required to track the progress to full attendance. Those responsible for this step will be, at times, reactive to the responses of the participants, and will also be, at times, proactive—prompting a commitment.

As RSVP's come in, additional information about the event may also need to be shared, and questions answered. Details about the speaker or the activity, or the length of time the event will take, are commonly requested; as well, policies regarding late arrivals or the attendance of children/babies may need to be established prior to this step.

During the RSVP process, the organizer will need to subtly and skillfully manage the allocation of tickets to the respondents based upon pre-established criteria related to participant segmentation. For example, if an existing superior client calls to request two tickets, the organizer may want to encourage that respondent to bring some guests (unidentified prospects) of their own:

> *"Mrs. Smith, I am delighted that you and Mr. Smith are available that evening. We have actually reserved a total of six tickets for you, in the hopes that you would like to bring a friend or relative. Shall I send you six tickets?"*

As the RSVP process unfolds, the organizer may need to adjust the generosity of the ticket allocation. If the response is strong, and the attendance seems to be nearing capacity, the organizer may need to reduce the allocation of those extra tickets; on the other hand, if the response suggests that it will be difficult to achieve maximum capacity, the organizer may want to offer additional tickets to other (less superior) clients that he or she may not have otherwise made the offer to.

As participants become experienced with the events, they will be more inclined to request the opportunity to bring a guest (without being prompted). As such, event organizers may need to factor such possibilities into the attendance projections, and should also be prepared to politely restrict the ticket allocation if required or desired:

> *"Mr. Davis, I am delighted to hear that your children are also interested in attending the event, unfortunately the seating is limited, and the interest has been very positive, so we cannot accommodate any more guests at this time. I have started a waiting list, and will let you know if we have any cancellations".*

To be effective in making such ticket allocation determinations, the designated RSVP manager will need to establish a communications record to track the process; this will likely start with the full list of segmented participants. For example:

Name	Type*	Invitation Sent	RSVP	Tickets:		
				allocated	requested	sent
Smith	Superior	Yes	Yes	6	6	6
Brown	Moderate	Yes	Yes	2	4	4
Jones	Superior	Yes	Yes	4	2	2
Davis	Moderate	Yes	Yes	2	6	2
Harris	Moderate	Yes	Yes	2	0	0

*Type refers to the results of participant segmentation

Managing the RSVP process in this way allows the organizer to effectively monitor the delivery of tickets relative to the number available and the allocation guide. It will prompt the organizer when a proactive follow up is required (by lack of RSVP), and it will allow them to recognize when adjustments are required. With the above, for example, the organizer has only committed 14 tickets, when (by the allocation guide) 16 were available, and 18 were requested. At this rate, the event will be under-subscribed, and the RSVP manager should be more generous with the distribution.

By requiring an RSVP, as opposed to merely sending an invitation, or merely sending tickets, the host of the event can attempt to ensure that, first, all of the seats are filled, and, second, that the better positive relationships, and their unidentified prospects, are taking up as many of those seats as demand will permit. Moreover, by asking the participant to respond and request tickets, the organizer is dramatically increasing the likelihood that the responding participant will actually attend.

"How many tickets would you like?" is known, in sales vernacular, as a *minor point close.* By answering this question, the target market is making a commitment to the communicator, and, again, the likelihood of attendance increases.

| The purpose of Step #3, The RSVP | **To have participants confirm the desired number of tickets, Step #4.** |

The professional or business owner (or group thereof) organizing the event should consider their level of involvement in the RSVP process.

This determination will be influenced by factors such as the number of participants to be touched by the communications strategy, the maximum guest capacity of the venue, and the size of the support team. A lawyer, accountant, financial advisor, doctor, etc., for example, may find it impractical, or impossible, to proactively reach out to each invitee with an extra encouragement of attendance; conversely, to delegate *all* of that relationship-building opportunity away to staff or associates is almost always a mistake as well. I have found it best to identify some of the most significant of the positive relationships (the most superior of clients, or the best source of referrals, etc), or the most interesting of identified prospects (a local celebrity, or politician, perhaps), with a very personalized invitation *in addition to* the one being mailed or delivered. This may be in the form of an additional letter or phone call:

"Hello, Bob. You may have already received the invitation to our upcoming special event, but I want to personally follow up and let you know how much I have appreciated having you as a client this past year, and would really welcome the opportunity to tell you in person at the event. How many tickets would you like?"

Or...

"Hello Mayor Smith, you may not remember me; we met last month at the Chamber of Commerce lunch. An invitation has been sent to you for our upcoming special event. If you are available, I would like you to attend as our guest of honour. Shall I have my assistant deliver a couple of tickets to your office?"

A second notable opportunity for involvement by the event organizing professional is a proactive communication effort to the local media (if relevant). Though the identified media targets would have also received an invitation, some additional prompting could be most useful. This might be in the form of a news release (additional information that further stimulates interest), or an offer by the organizer to provide the event's featured speaker for an interview, or perhaps even letting it slip that the mayor has requested a couple of tickets. By engaging the media directly, the host may find themselves as part of the reported story—complete with pictures and quotes.

A relationship with dignitaries, notables and the media may not happen easily and quickly, with the very first event. Over time, however, as the reputation of the organizers within the community grows, so will these, potentially very significant, relationships.

Step #4: The Tickets

The final communication step before the event is the delivering of the tickets and any additional information (like a map, or parking instructions) that the attending participant may find useful. Whether or not the tickets would actually be required to enter the venue is wholly irrelevant; indeed, ideally, the tickets should be retained by the guests, and not even be collected by the host.

Though providing a modest amount of information (confirming date, time, location, etc), the impact of the ticket comes more from its form. As with the invitation, it should reinforce the recipient's interest in the activity and the venue, perhaps with a bold statement of the event: "African Safari Adventure!", for example. It also offers the organizer the opportunity to creatively extend the theme of the event in its design, and it should, of course, exist in three dimensions in the hopes that it will be posted on the fridge (next to the invitation).

Some venues provide ticket printing and design services—complete with organizer name, and company logo if desired. I have even used *Ticketmaster* when trying to establish a more formal, classic communications program, but the tickets need not conform to the stereotype to be effective. Depending on the event, variations on the theme can be explored. Perhaps a "back stage pass" would be appropriate for a theatrical performance, or a musical instrument museum (like Cantos). A "boarding pass" could be used for a Pirate Ship, or some other travel related event activity, while "a letter granting permission to enter" could be presented by a guest when entering an exclusive facility (like the Canadian Mint). A few years ago, I was exploring Washington DC for potential venues and came across a *Spy Museum*; perhaps guests would require "assignment papers" to attend an awesome client event there.

Despite the range of design and expressive opportunities, one thing that every ticket *should* have in common is an indication of ticket price or admission fee.

 The purpose of Step #4, The Tickets   **Communicate a statement of value.**

By having a price clearly indicated on the ticket, pass, etc, the organizer is pointing out to the guests that participation in the venue and activity has an associated value—even if the guest is never actually asked to pay that price. The amount of the indicated fee need not reflect the actual per person cost to the host, but is more likely to represent what would be charged under circumstances where a reasonable profit was being pursued by a professional event planner.

Upon requesting, and then receiving six tickets, the respondent comes to be in possession of $210 worth of activity and venue—which is then posted on the fridge. A social contract is formed, and most participants will feel morally bound to attend the event (with friends or family) as promised. On those rare occasions when the guest is subsequently unable to fulfill their obligation, they will be far more inclined to distribute those tickets to other friends and family; they gain the opportunity to generously give $210 worth of event, and ensure that their equally generous host is not *out* the $210 worth of obvious effort. The host has an opportunity to initiate a new relationship with unidentified prospects now attending the event, while still *touching* those relationships initially targeted with the tickets.

The tickets and their statement of value may also attract other participants, such as the paying public and the media. A couple of years ago, I helped to organize an event for a financial services professional, with myself as the featured speaker. The communications process was followed, and tickets were distributed. A local radio personality heard about the event, learned about the "valuable" tickets, and contacted me with an offer: if we were prepared to give the radio station some tickets (as give-a-ways for their listening audience), and if I conceded to be interviewed for content and a series of promotional spots, then the radio station would provide commercial time for free. I was definitely prepared, and happily agreed to their terms.

Event organizers can also use such valuable tickets to extend an offer to their identified intermediaries: those centres-of-influences that can motivate unidentified prospects to attend the event. The host could approach, for example, other professionals with whom they have positive relationships, and from whom they might reasonably expect to receive referrals (or, at least, introductions) with the following:

> *"Jane, I would like to show my appreciation to you for the referrals you have given to me over the past year; so here are 20 tickets to a very exciting event that we have organized. You are welcome to distribute these to your friends and clients as you deem appropriate."*

Jane is now empowered with $1000 worth of excitement, and she can use that as her own relationship-building opportunity. Under these circumstances, the host would be wise to pursue an introduction to those, now identified, prospective clients at the event. Moreover, if Jane comes to find relationship-building value from the experience, she may be inclined to accept a more significant role (perhaps as event partner) with future activities.

One of the very popular "Retire to Mexico" events was held in Cranbrook, BC, for a family that develops recreational property in (of all places) Mazatlan, Mexico. Their objective was to show appreciation to the current clients, but also attract the attention of some others. Perhaps used to considering relatively expensive marketing campaigns, the family had prepared a budget which would include a healthy allocation to local newspaper advertisement, to help promote the event. After some consulting, I encouraged them to simply create tickets with an attractive price, and approach their most significant indentified intermediaries, with an offer of ten to twenty tickets each as gifts for *their* clients. Very shortly, those tickets were distributed, and a commitment of 150 attendees was secured—which brought the largest available venue to capacity. The newspaper advertisement campaign became redundant, and was immediately cancelled. By presenting a statement value to the participants, the actual cost of the event was dramatically reduced.

Step #5: Addressing the Attendees

By the date and time of the event, the hosts and team of organizers anxiously await the arrival of the guests. Much effort and energy has been invested in the process, from identifying the participants, to organizing the venue and activity, and implementing a communications program. Anticipation had been aroused by the buzz, and guests had been prompted to RSVP by the invitation; tickets have been requested, and received. If the steps have been implemented effectively, participants fulfill their obligation and arrive -eager to enjoy the promised value.

As the venue fills, organizers may become relaxed, confident that the proceedings are unfolding as planned, and perhaps even self-congratulatory. However, the host's responsibilities are far from over; the purpose of all the planning was not merely to entice attendance, but to provide the opportunity for an experience in support of relationship-building objectives. As such, the organizer must not be lulled into passivity, nor adopt the role of an observer, but must actively capitalize on the opportunities to engage the participants. They must truly embrace the role of host.

The first duty is ensure some form of welcoming as the guests arrive to the immediate vicinity of the venue. Depending upon the specific physical layout, attendants (or signs) may be required in the parking lot, or at an entrance gate, or in a lobby, or at one or more doors, to provide a friendly smile, confirmation, and some additional directions. Typically, a reception table would also be arranged very close to the primary location of the activity, where tickets could be checked, and, perhaps, attendance taken. Each member of the organizing team should participate at some stage of the welcoming.

As the formal activities of the event begin, a designated host will be required to verbally address the guests. The purpose is to provide a self-introduction, officially welcome the group, review how the event will unfold, how long it will take, and offer polite reminders regarding cell phones, talking, etc. This would also be the appropriate time to acknowledge special guests, dignitaries and notables in attendance. Very importantly, the designated host may be required to deliver an introduction of a speaker or a person over-seeing the event activities. As the positioning of a speaker or performer to an audience with a professional and effective introduction can greatly influence that audience's experience of the event, and, as such, speakers and performers would expect no less, the host, or a capable representative, should be amply prepared for this duty.

Customarily, often at or near the end of the event, the host will acknowledge and thank more significantly contributing participants to the entire audience. Such participants may include the organizing team, event partners and sponsors, the caterer, and especially the draw speaker, entertainer, guide, activity provider, etc. In particular, and often in closing, the host or hosts should take a moment to address the guests—those existing and potential relationships— with a sincere and special message:

> *"Ladies and gentlemen, I want to take this opportunity to thank all of you for attending the event. Our business/practice is successful and enjoyable because of each of you. On behalf of my colleagues and my team at ABC Ltd., we look forward to serving all of you, your friends, and family, in the future. Good night and drive safely".*

That final address may support the underlying, specific objectives of the host regarding the event (retention, referrals, recruiting, succession, etc), but, ultimately, the special message is the opportunity for the host to touch the audience, and express in words what the event is to have expressed in action: that the relationships are recognized and valued.

The purpose of Step #5, Address	**Emotionally connect with the guests.**

THE BIGGEST, MOST COMMON MISTAKE...

When it comes to the communication process, the biggest common mistake is that the organizer adopts a "build-it-and-they-will-come" attitude. They assume that, with very little marketing effort, participants will flock to the venue for the activity. Organizers must remember that the target market is already overloaded with information, and that the desired action will require multiple communication steps, executed with care, patience and diligence. An obvious effort is required.

A TIP TO REDUCE COSTS...

Experienced event enthusiasts will look to the venue representative and/or the activity representatives to provide graphic design and printing services and support. As an added value to their service, and in the hopes of contributing to a successful experience, such representatives may have pre-prepared invitations and/or tickets available, with the ability to personalize those for the specific event. Such stock communication pieces are particularly prevalent for larger events, where communication pieces are often created for a general, public audience and for activities which feature travel experiences. In many cases, well-chosen event sponsors may already have available, or will prepare as part of their support as sponsor, communication pieces—especially if those pieces also recognize and promote the sponsor.

ACTION STEPS AND SCHEDULE ...

Create buzz	1 year to 2 months prior
Confirm venue and activity	3 months prior
Design and print invitations and tickets	3—2 months prior
Design RSVP tracking system	7 weeks prior
Send invitations	6—5 weeks prior
RSVP process, and follow-up	4—3 weeks prior
Media, dignitary contact	3 weeks prior
Send tickets	3—2 weeks prior
Event "walk-through" (including caterer, equipment, signs, parking, bathrooms, etc)	1 week prior
Prepare speeches	1 week prior

Include:

- self-introduction and introduction of co-hosts
- welcome guests
- acknowledge special guests
- review event (what's going to happen)
- polite reminders
- introduction of speaker, activity provider
- thank speaker, activity provider upon completion
- thank other supporting participants, sponsors
- special message to guests

FOURTH COMPONENT: LASTING MEMORIES

L*asting Memories* are those initiatives that serve to remind the participants, not only of the event, the obvious effort, and motivations, but especially of those related positive relationships. As such, they are a form of continuing communication to the participants. In similarity with those other communication pieces that are more effective in three dimensions (rather than the two-dimensional, electronic copies), *lasting memories* can be thought as adding effectiveness with the addition of a dimension to the communications strategy: the dimension of time.

Such fourth dimensional communication pieces are those that the participants *take away* with them, after the event, or prompt future fond recollections. These are the elements that elevate the experience from being of minor and fleeting significance, to a more substantial, longer-term, and bonding memory-maker. Over time, the totality of these pieces will serve to establish and support the business or practice brand, and may contribute substantially to its value.

Relative to the other key components, *lasting memories* are most likely to be an after-thought—if they are considered at all. Upon reflection, seasoned and inexperienced event organizers alike will recognize that the first three components (participants, venue/activity and communications) *must* be addressed in some way if there is to be a relationship-building experience at all. Those elements of an event, however, that extend that experience into the future, though perhaps optional, are a critical component for the full realization of the event's purpose and potential.

Pictures

A relatively easy way to initiate some *lasting memories* into an awesome client event is by taking, and sending, pictures. This tactic can be approached by simply designating an event photographer to capture the experiences as the proceeding unfold, and ensure that the images are then shared and otherwise used to extend those experiences.

When I first began to employ event planning within my practice, photographs were still taken, developed, and mailed the "old fashioned" way, with processes and technology that had not changed dramatically in decades. What began as a definite art form of painted portraits of the wealthy, by the extraordinarily talented, has slowly evolved into still black and white photographic portraits of special events (weddings, holidays, etc) by those that could afford the equipment, and then into a plethora of colour electronic pictures, snapped, posted and shared at the speed of light by almost everyone.

Along the way, consistent with the principles of supply and demand, as the availability of the still image has increased, their general value seems to have decreased. There was a time, when taking a picture was done carefully and thoughtfully, because, after all, the rolls of film offered only a limited number of opportunities, and there was a cost associated with developing every picture—even those that were blurry or just badly framed. Today, technology ensures that there is no limit to the number of pictures that can be taken, and either very quickly deleted, or altered to the desired form. As a result, the value of an image is plummeting.

With this in mind, if a picture from an event is to have value for the participant, it must attempt to capture and record a special, and perhaps unique, moment. It must serve to maintain a desirable memory for the guest. The advancements and applications of image technology have been most notable in leisure and travel pursuits, when the experiences are often fleeting. Rides and attractions, for example, from Disney World to Las Vegas, are increasingly concluded with an action picture and an opportunity for the subjects to purchase that image. One of my personal favorites features my wife and I riding in a wicker basket/toboggan, with two Venetian-gon-dolier-like pilots driving dog-sled style, down the very steep, narrow, and winding streets of a mountain-top village on an island off the coast of Africa. We were so caught up in the moment, laughing like children, and traveling so quickly, that taking our own picture was impossible; so when a picture of us "magically" appeared at the end of the ride, complete in a promotional folder, we were happy to pay the price.

Ensuring that the event provides suitable photo opportunities is the responsibility of the hosts, and should be considered during the organizational process. The interactive elements of the experience are often the most generous in this regard: a picture of a guest engaging in a leisure activity (learning to golf, or riding a horse, for example), or of a guest holding an exotic animal (a snake, or a parrot) at the zoo, or of a guest talking to a famous author or speaker, and so on.

A financial advisor from the Greater Toronto Area has been known to organize luncheons featuring a fashion show for entertainment; the twist, though, is that the guests (her clients) become the models and strut on the runway. As one might imagine, this provides numerous opportunities for action pictures, and they are most likely to be kept by the models.

After the event, guests can be presented with a picture of themselves, and a note of "thanks for attending"; for those that did not manage to make it into a picture themselves, a general image of the event, like a post card, may be appropriate.

Events that include travel may be the most significant provider of photo opportunities: holiday pictures seem to be among the most commonly taken, and most likely to be retained. At the Pirate Ship Adventure in Cancun, for example, while the guests were boarding the ship, pictures were taken of them with the Mexican Pirates; by the time the festivities were completed, and the ship returned to dock, the pictures were framed and distributed to the guests as they disembarked. In addition to that, my adult children and my wife took pictures of all the guests as they partied; these were combined with dozens of pictures from the resort, and other activities associated with the trip, organized into a slide show presentation, set to music, and distributed to all guests on a disc soon after the group had returned to Canada. While creating *lasting memories* for 150 guests, we were creating some wonderful *lasting memories* for our family as well.

Gifts and Books

A second type of keepsake for a guest could be in the form of a modest gift. In preparation for the African Safari Adventure, for example, I contacted the Calgary Zoo to determine if they could recommend one of their retail products for a bulk purchase. They offered the remaining supply of (recently discontinued) stuffed, furry, black gorillas. Though the price to me was already well below retail, I contacted a lawyer and an accountant, with whom I had been sharing referrals, with the following offer:

> *"I am hosting a client event, and I would like you to attend. By the way, I would also like you to pay for a gift for each of the guests: stuffed, baby black gorillas with your business card on a red ribbon, tied around its neck."*

Hesitantly, they both agreed, and on the evening of the event, posted at each exit, were my assistants with big baskets of these adorable baby gorillas and red ribbons. On their way out, guests would

receive their gifts, so my closing remarks—the special message—
included:

> *"Finally, ladies and gentleman, I have one more surprise for you.*
> *Many of you may already have met, or are already working with,*
> *our preferred lawyer and accountant. I would like them to be rec-*
> *ognized—please stand up gentlemen. They have provided a gift*
> *for each of you as a token of their appreciation. You will receive*
> *that on your way out; thank-you, again, and good night".*

Both the accountant and the lawyer were pleased with the resulting business opportunities, and were eager to participate in future
events.

When it comes to achieving a truly *lasting memory* and impact,
books are particularly effective gifts; they are mostly likely to be
kept, collected, treasured and the bequeathed—especially when
they are signed by the author. One of the reasons that I have fa-
voured the participation of speakers and writers for client events
is that they almost always have a book available. Not only do the
books become part of the guest's library, they also become the hid-
ing place for the event tickets, invitations and pictures: another reason that communication pieces should exist in three dimensions!

As I write this, I can see my own collection—books that I have kept
from so many events that I have enjoyed and organized: each of them
presented by, and signed by, the author. The topics are surprisingly
varied: adventure books by the likes of Goodall and Kirkby; biogra-
phies from Rubin "Hurricane" Carter and Frank Abagnale (played

by Leonardo Dicaprio in *Catch Me If You Can*); Canadian Olympic gold medal winner, Mark Tewksbury; business-related books, including Mennis' *Average To Awesome*, and Chilton's *Wealthy Barber*; Chopra's *How To Know God*, and *Unlikely Utopia* by Michael Adams. Despite this variety, they have something in common: they represent, for me, a connection to an experience that I do not want to forget.

I know that, as these books stir my *lasting memories*, so they will for others, my many guests and clients, who have enjoyed the awesome events. I also know, from the referrals of new relationships, that those books are conversation starters; a relative or friend, visiting the home of one of those clients, will pick up a book, have a look, see the pictures and signatures, and then pick up another, and another.

"How is it that you have meet these famous people?", they may ask.

"My financial advisor introduced me at a client event", may be the response.

The Experience

A particularly interesting or enjoyable activity can also provide a *lasting memory* for the guests, even without reminders such as pictures and gifts. These might be in the form of some highly engaging and unusual leisure experience, or an activity that promoted learning and personal growth. Better professional speakers, for example, offer messages that can have a long-term impact on the audience: unforgettable stories, motivation, and insight, with such an entertaining delivery, that the guests are often inspired to be better themselves.

The primary purpose behind the "Adventures in Retirement" keynote presentations was to motivate and inspire retirees and pre-retirees to think about, and plan for, the amazing opportunities that are available to them as they transition from a life characterized by work and parenting responsibilities, to a life characterized more-or-less by leisure. The hope is that the audience would approach this coming time of their life with confidence, some imagination and a sense of adventure—to make the most of the time still available. Moreover, the "Retire to Mexico!" seminars, in continuation of the theme, provided specific information and details about adventurous Canadians that were pursuing their retirement dreams in exotic destinations; the guests learned where these retirees were living and about their quality of life. As travel events were subsequently organized, guests were also able to experience, first hand, the locations and lifestyles of the snowbirds and expatriates.

I feel fortunate, not only that I was able to create and deliver these messages, but that I am now able to experience the results—as measured by the choices made by some of those in the audience; very regularly, for example, I will hear from one of these guests that they have purchased a second home, for the winter, and are very excited about how their life is unfolding.

As well, the host can also greatly benefit from, and be inspired by, the experience of the event. Cecile Wyatt, a very successful financial advisor in Regina, Saskatchewan, had built her practice, and maintained her relationships, with awesome client events. As she was helping her clients to prepare for and pursue their retirement plans, she was planning her own adventures in retirement; she has recently invited me to provide a "Retire to Mexico!" seminar for her clients, as part of her strategy of introducing her successor, so that she can now fulfill her dream of travelling and exploring the world.

The *lasting memory* created by a professional speaker can also come in the form of a very humorous surprise. The African Safari event, for example, treated the audience to music, video, and a keynote presentation by the remarkably charming, informative and entertaining Brian Keating. The presentations began dramatically: the lights went off, and the rhythmic sounds of African drums filled the darkness, effectively transporting the guests to the banks of the Zambezi River. As the video began, Keating provided narration, and the story of a recent expedition that he had organized, for a group of Canadians (mostly, seniors), unfolded. Periodically, the guests were brought to the edge of their seat by the sudden presence and sound of exotic and menacing wild-life. At a moment of deceptive calm, the video offers an image of Keating, enjoying a well-earned rest after a day's journey, playfully cart-wheeling down a hill into the river, and he is completely naked! As if to satisfy the eye-rubbing disbelief of the audience, again drawn to the edge of their seat, the scene repeats immediately, and Keating's "playfulness" is unmistakably confirmed by a telling silhouette against the crimson sunset. This wholly unexpected disclosure would become one of the most talked about, and laughed about, aspects of any of the awesome events.

Great seriousness can also be a most memorable and impactful element of a powerful speaker's presentation. Jane Goodall captivated two thousand guests, in a most unusual way, at an event in Oct 2001. Her popularity had arisen, in part, from a presentation style that featured story-telling against a back-drop of beautiful photographs; the adventure tales, and the characters, brought to life by the remarkable images (primarily) of chimpanzees and their habitat. So associated is she with her pictures, that to appear at an event without them would be akin to Elton John performing without a piano. And yet, there she was on stage, with an audience in eager anticipation, and *without* her images.

Jane disclosed to everyone that she had been dramatically impacted be events in New York on September 11th. Her slide presentation had been at her office close to the twin towers, and she could not access them for the event. She detailed her experience of the tragedy and discussed the lasting impact that it might have on the world. While enough time had passed since the attack to allow for philosophical reflections, wounds had not healed, and her message tapped into a dark and deep shared melancholy, and resonated profoundly with everyone. After the event, Jane sent me a note with the words:

"Together we can make this a better world for all".

This, I believe, is much more than a hope or a wish, and even more than a statement of fact; it is a challenge. Her *lasting memory* was to inspire the guests to consider how to make a difference in the lives of others, and in the health of the planet. As the host, I realized that an event can be a forum to address the often-troubling issues of the day, and a powerful tool that influences awareness, thought, and perhaps action.

Branding the Office

Long after an event has concluded, and the organizers and guests are again busy with the (perhaps comparatively mundane) regular activities of work, an excellent opportunity remains for fourth dimensional communications. The physical environment of the business and professional services, where staff, clients and prospects interact—the office, the board room, the shop, the reception area, connecting halls and corridors, and even the bathrooms —are a typically vastly underutilized canvas for *lasting memories*.

Often these facilities languish as merely reinforcing the stereotype of the related profession or business: old and tired magazines, sales awards, acknowledgements of education and training, images of products provided, and services rendered. Or the space is surrendered to bad art, cliché motivational posters, and the stuff (like sports memorabilia) that the owners want to treat as a business expense before relocating to the family room at home.

Affirming the old adage that "you cannot *not* communicate" the work environment is communicating to the current and potential relationships. It might be saying that in this location a particular product is sold, or a particular service is provided; unfortunately, many products and services are not actually desired in and of themselves but are seen by the clients as a means to an end, or, worse, a necessary evil, and, at any rate, are being offered by countless others. Or the work environment might be saying that those of us practicing or conducting business here are not particularly interesting or imaginative, and are prepared to accept a state undifferentiated mediocrity.

On the other hand, those premises *could be* used to reaffirm a relationship, and serve to remind of a shared experience and history. Many top-performers effectively establish differentiation, and build their personal or practice brand, by applying the philosophy and principles of *lasting memories* where they work. As I have travelled across Canada, both learning from and coaching various professionals, I have taken the opportunity—whenever possible—to tour their premises in search of physical manifestations of character and personality. Though rare, those that are adept in this regard certainly succeed in making an impression.

The successful financial planner in Kamloops, BC, (see Participants: Identified and Unidentified Prospects), had only one picture in his office, and it filled an entire wall: he and his wife on a Harley motorcycle. The image not only expressed his personality and interests, it reminded guests of his fund-raising events and social involvements. In support of his value proposition and brand affirmation, the motorcycle is a metaphor for "freedom", and, perhaps, "rebellion". The investment advice he offers is not the needed or desired end in itself, but it is only the means to the true objective: *financial* freedom.

A more significant opportunity for *lasting memories* in the office environment becomes available when an entire firm, partnership, or collective of professionals, collaborate on the relationship-building, event planning, and branding efforts. One of my favorite examples is an Investors Group office in Burnaby, BC. This group of advisors, managers and support staff had been supporting the local vibrant performing arts community by sponsoring musical theatre performances as activity/venue combinations for awesome client events. Promotional posters were framed and hung in the premises, as a *lasting memory* of previous events and a buzz for those up-coming. Staff and existing clients are provided with fond reminders when they visit the office, while prospective clients and potential new advisors receive the message that this particular office is unique, and dedicated to community involvement.

Dr. Chris Oswald is a nationally known and award-winning chiropractor, author and educator based in Southern Ontario. His relationship-building events are often very physical and active, including long-distance cycling. Photographs capture the shared experiences and are proudly displayed in his reception area, not only as *lasting memories,* but in recognition of a simple truth: clients do not come to him because they desire a treatment or an adjustment, but because they desire the *active lifestyle* that can result from being physically able. So the images remind existing and prospective clients of the true value and benefit of the services—the desired ends—rather than the perhaps less-than-desirable means. (More on Dr Oswald in Part Three)

Pictures, gifts and books that were used as *lasting memories* for the event participants, can also be used in the work environment. A photo-album for each event, complete with news-clippings, tickets, invitations, programs, postcards, boarding passes, etc, could replace the magazines in the reception area, while those autographed books could come to fill the shelf of a central office or popular meeting room. Pictures of featured speakers, dignitaries, and guests in action, could be blown up, mounted and framed for lobbies, hallways and boardrooms.

My personal favorite form of creating *lasting memories* was to have posters signed and dated by guest speakers, then mounted with tickets and invitations, and hung in my primary office. These were often promotional pieces, with the name of the draw attraction, the title of the presentation, very colourful and professionally designed, and with a personalized message to me of "thanks", "congratulations", or the like. Visiting clients would be reminded of these, often famous, people, whom they had met at an event, and fond reminiscing would follow:

"How *is* Bruce Kirkby? ", they might inquire, as if of an old friend.

Such discourse often led to conversational buzz regarding an upcoming event, and a request from the client that I include a particular friend or relative on the guest list—a person that they really want me to meet.

Another consequence—wholly unexpected and unforeseen—of the awesome client events that took a physical form in the office was the growing number of thank-you cards, from delighted guests, standing on the credenza and pinned to the bulletin board. Sadly, the age of electronic communications seems to be ushering in the demise of such gentle politeness.

THE BIGGEST, MOST COMMON MISTAKE...

Event organizers and hosts are often so focused on the specific date of the event, the specific activity and venue, and the myriad details to be attended to, that they may forget altogether about addressing elements of *lasting memories*. Can you imagine planning and attending your son or daughter's wedding, or embarking on a 25th anniversary Mediterranean cruise, and *not* taking pictures or video and *not* buying souvenirs? The effort to commemorate an event confirms the importance of that event; it serves to form and maintain the relationship bonds of the participants, and it is the catalyst for communicating to others.

A TIP TO REDUCE COSTS...

Having organized the venue and activity, and achieved attendance objectives, that added cost and effort associated with recording the event with pictures is most insignificant. Though the host cannot know with certainty that images shared with the guests are ever seen or referred to again, pictures that are turned into brand-reinforcing, and relationship-reinforcing *lasting memories*, and come to be an integral part of the office and work environment, are a most cost-effective form of fourth-dimension communications.

ACTION STEPS...

Arrange gifts, books, etc, as determined	6 to 1 month prior
Arrange for photographer/videographer	1 month prior
Strategize photo opportunities (during event "walk through")	1 week prior
Distribute *lasting memories* to guests	date of the event to 2 weeks after
Add *lasting memories* to office/web site	within 1 month after

SUMMARY

The value of recognizing and understanding the four key components, and the myriad related decisions to be made and details to be addressed, is twofold. First, it empowers the organizer with an ability to identify and perform a particular set of tasks, in a particular way, within a particular process or order, and with an appreciation of how those tasks are meant to fulfill the objectives. An individual that is fully responsible for the planning of an event can follow the recipe: participants, venue/activity, communications and lasting memories.

Second, it provides the means for the creation of, and implementation of, a systematized approach. Those that recognize the importance of relationship-building for the success of a business or practice may be working as part of a team, or within a partnership or professional collective, or may be leading or managing that collective; as such, that person may need to work as a group, or organize and direct others, to architect the awesome event. In this environment, it is of critical importance that each organizing participant understands their assigned role and related tasks, but also how that effort relates to and supports the other members of the group.

Through systematization also comes the ability to replicate the efforts over time. Event planning can become a regular function of business operations, to the point that it is recognizable as an element of the corporate culture, or practice/business personality, character, and brand.

A systematized approach can also assist in relating the desired, measurable results back to specific tasks and performers. Those quantifiable aspects of the business, such as client retention, new client acquisition, human resource development/recruiting, etc., will be monitored, and the role of the awesome events in those changing state of affairs can be determined. As results are measured relative to objectives, or as the objectives are altered in response to the needs or circumstances of the business, the event planner can identify the individual tasks for alteration and adjustment, and the performers for coaching and support.

If, for example, new client acquisition and prospect referrals are not meeting expectations, the efforts related to participants may be addressed by increasing the allocation of tickets to superior existing clients. Or if RSVP results are slow, the activities regarding the invitation, or choices regarding the venue, may need to be assessed.

To assist in the determination of a particular event's success, especially during the inaugural effort, a proactive approach may be of value. This can be in the form of a request for feedback or a questionnaire, provided at the event itself, or as part of a post-event review—perhaps with the sending of pictures, etc. If a guest is invited to provide feedback at the event, that process should be as easy and as simple as is necessary to fulfill the need.

Though part of a process, the event planning activities need not *feel* as such for the organizers; rather, they can be a welcomed break from more tedious duties, and a wonderful opportunity for creativity. As well, the hosts must ensure that the guests, and other non-organizing participants, do not come to feel as if *they* are part of a process. A system which includes imagination, variety, sincerity, and a spirit of generosity, can both be efficient in its process and effective in its relationship-building purpose.

The participants, venue/activity, communications and lasting memories are brought together, not merely to fill some business function, or to address some profit-related objective, but to provide *all* of those involved with an opportunity to bring personal growth, pleasure, excitement and adventure to their lives.

PART THREE

3

PREFACE

More than a decade ago, as I was planning my very first event, I realized that I would need some guidance. I was most fortunate to discover a number of clever, talented, and successful professionals and business owners whose excellence in relationship-building was matched by their generosity in sharing their secrets and strategies.

In their hands, the four key components of an awesome client event are reassembled in a variety of creative and inspiring ways.

Part Three will focus on a few of these top-performers, and tell their stories of success. I have attempted to provide an interesting mix of examples: older and more recent events, various geographic locations with differing economic environments, representation from various professions and industries, and reflecting differing objectives and ambitions.

At first glance, these examples seem to be far more dissimilar than similar. However, when viewed against a back-drop of broader demographic and social trends, not only do the striking commonalities become apparent, but one may begin to predict how the features of client events may continue to evolve.

Let us consider, first, this context, so that the work of the exemplars may be fully appreciated, and so each may serve as both muse and motivator.

Trend: Travel Activities

Once the basic needs of life are satisfied, humans pursue and enjoy an often bewildering array of interests and desires. Predicting how these pursuits will trend and become popular can be as valuable as it is difficult, but a common and elementary starting point for would-be prognosticators is a consideration of demographics. Specifically, one can hypothesize what trends will emerge in an aging population of so-called baby boomers.

From social scientists, to economists and entrepreneurs, many have assessed and studied the post second world war population increase (especially in North America) in an attempt to account for and explain a wide range of experiences, phenomena and data. A basic premise seems to underpin the resulting assertions: that, as baby boomers have aged, and moved en masse through the typical transition points of life, correspondingly, the needs, interests and desires have changed along the way. The resulting *demand* for related products and services fluctuate, with an effect on their *supply* and *price*. With this starting point, one might explain the introduction of and popularization of television and fast food restaurants, or changing automobile designs and suburban expansion, or the changing tastes of fashion and music in the 1960's, or the varying prices of stock markets and interest rates, or the rising costs of health care, etc.

Business persons, professionals and entrepreneurs have found in these myriad changes the opportunity to satisfy the needs, interests and desires of the baby boomers with products and services for mutual benefit. Indeed, many of you may have contemplated such opportunities when entering your chosen industry or profession, or may have adjusted your offering of products and services in light of developments related to demographics.

Baby boomers, as a cohort, are currently in the early stages of another, and very significant, change. The next twenty years will see them transition from a lifestyle that features employment—with the associated characteristics of responsibility, structure, and inflexibility—towards a lifestyle that will increasingly feature leisure pursuits. The commonly used, though typically undefined, term for this period is "retirement". This particular transition, and resulting stage of life, may well stand significantly apart from the others as a *new* human experience. Whereas other more-or-less recognizable and definable periods of our life (childhood, adolescence, becoming a parent, caring for a family, etc) have always been the normal part of the human experience, this coming, potentially protracted period of leisure is a brand new aspect of life.

It has been argued that the contemporary notion of "retirement" began with the introduction of a pension in Europe in the 1800's. The development of this notion subsequently occurred in North America in conjunction with other important developments, including: the introduction of our own pensions, increasing life-expectancy, improving quality of life related to health, financial services and support, and communications and transportation technologies. In short, for the first time in history, groups of people are living long enough, well enough, and with sufficient resources to allow them to pursue a lifestyle that would have been almost unimaginable for almost everyone else that has every lived.

As with other significant transitions, baby boomers are likely to express new and growing interests, desires and demands, many of which may be anticipated. Though, as a new feature of human life, this potentially long period of relative leisure may also produce some unexpected and surprising results (which may well provide unusual opportunity for the insightful and savvy entrepreneur). However, one trend that is worth considering is the rising interest in leisure pursuits related to travel.

A great number of my public speaking engagements over the last ten years have been for an audience of the general public—predominantly baby boomers—on topics related to retirement. At every opportunity, I have engaged the attendees to perform the following thought experiment: imagine that you are in a room filled with the recently retired and soon-to-be retired and all of you are asked to write down the top ten things you want to do before you die. How many of those items on the list are related to travel?

This admittedly unscientific research nevertheless produces very consistent results. As expected, the number out of ten is high: 7, 8, or 9. However, when discussed a little further, some of the other listed non-travel goals, ultimately prove to have a strong connection with travel. A goal of "spending more time with the grand kids", for example, is realized on a trip to a theme park or on a cruise; while a goal of "learning to speak another language" is ultimately realized as exclusively speaking Spanish during an extended living experience in Mexico.

As unsurprising as the results of these audience engagements and thought experiments might be, the implications can be useful. For example, despite the fact that a large and identifiable portion of our population has the time, resources and disposition to pursue some of the most important goals of their life, relatively few business and professionals seek to capitalize on that information, by offering value through related products and service. Indeed, and quite to the contrary, what most of us offer will never show up on that list of "top-ten things to do before I die", nor are we likely to be inclined or able to alter our core business activity to address that fact.

However, and to the point, we *can* alter our processes, and, in fact, I believe a clear indication of this can be seen in recent trends regarding relationship-building and awesome client events. Since the publication of the first edition of this book, the essence of the client event activities, especially among the leaders and top-performers, seems to be evolving from *mock* adventures to *real* adventures, or from *escapism* to actually escaping, or from an appreciation of, and entertainment from, someone else's life changing experience to realization of one's *own* life changing experience.

This development may represent a natural progression of a practice or business strategy that has been forced to improve by client expectations, increasing competition among event planning enthusiasts, and the natural tendency among top-performers towards an ever raising bar of business goals and standards. As well, these developments may be an indication of the professional and business owner's insightfulness and sensitivity to the changing desires of their aging clients, coupled with their natural relationship-building instincts. However, I anticipate, and hope, that there is another significant contributing factor. The professionals and business owners that are organizing and hosting travel-related client events are often aging baby boomers themselves. As with the rest of their cohort, they have their own personal goals and adventures to pursue: their own "list of things to do before I die". Such travel-related events represent an opportunity for those folk to realize some of their lifestyle objectives, and include friends, family and countless other positive relationships.

Four Key Components for Travel Events

Client events that feature a travel activity present a host of interesting planning challenges throughout the four key components, and, as with other types of client events, top-performers are proving to be most clever and creative. In addition to the general comments, descriptions, and explanations outlined in Part Two, travel events present a few different considerations, and come with specific attractions and short-comings.

Regarding participants, you should be aware that in most cases the organizer *is not* covering the cost for the guests. While in some cases, particularly large or successful businesses will treat a qualifying subset of their client base to a complimentary trip, many smaller businesses and practices (or larger businesses seeking to accomplish more while spending less), will expect their clients to cover the entire cost of the travel experience. The value or service the host is providing is the organization itself and related activity that will make that experience attractive. It is typical that other event stakeholders, such as partners and sponsors, will also cover their own costs and contribute to the success of the event.

An exception to this may be related to a draw speaker or entertainer; I have, for example, on a few occasions, enticed a keynote presenter on a travel experience with a promise of a free week on a cruise ship or at an all-inclusive resort. Typically, that "free" experience was made available to me, negotiated with the travel agent, based upon a volume of business or group booking. For example, each fifteen couples booked for a cruise may produce passage for one more couple with compliments:

"Mrs Jones, would you like the opportunity to speak on a cruise ship and promote your new book? While I cannot pay your usual fee, I can provide you with a complimentary holiday, for you and Mr Jones. Would you and he would like to join us?"

Honestly, I have never had anyone not want to do this.

Depending upon the nature of the activities or features related to the travel event, a great number of existing relationships, identified prospects, and unidentified prospects may also be inclined to participate. For example, a financial advisor that I interviewed in Edmonton, AB organized a "business fair" on a cruise ship for her self-employed clients, so that they could promote their services and network; they were encouraged to invite other self-employed business owners and professionals (that had not been identified by the organizer). The identified intermediaries encouraged the participation of those unidentified prospects, with whom their share referrals or collaborate on client needs. I have also interviewed an American financial advisor that focuses on the needs of dentists; he and his team organizes professional development conferences for his existing clients, and to meet other dentists (identified prospects, by virtue of belonging to an identifiable group that can be communicated to directly).

A new positive and significant relationship is likely to emerge from these planning efforts: the travel agent—whose expertise and guidance can be invaluable. Travel agents are often business owners and entrepreneurs as well, and can quickly realize, appreciate and support the relationship-building objectives of the host. Moreover, a clever travel agent will also become a stakeholder in the success of the event, in the hopes of providing value, earning future opportunities, and (where appropriate) promoting the travel event to their own clients, the general public, and even the media. Importantly, the travel agent will also relieve the event organizer of having to collect payments from clients and deal with their other, potentially personal, organization details.

With respect to the venue, arguably the easiest and most effective option is a larger facility with ample support, entertainment, food and beverage services: essentially, traditional travel venues. All-inclusive resorts and cruises ships, for example, are very organized, easy to arrange (both transportation and accommodations), provide meeting rooms, entertainment, excursions, and can accommodate the various needs and desires that come with a large group of travelers. Importantly, such traditional venues make it possible for individual/couple experiences as well as group experiences, and with sufficient selection of destinations to attract participants again and again. Though non-traditional venues in your community (as described earlier) provide for cost-effective novelty, and may be appropriate for relatively short experiences that the organizer is paying for, non-traditional venues for travel may represent a significant risk for the organizer, especially when longer activities occur and the clients are expected to pay.

While traditional travel venues tend to feature a wide variety of activities, suitable for all ages, interests and physical conditions that permit a high degree of interaction between all participants, event organizers routinely add special activities to the experience. Though often more passive in nature—speakers, seminars, etc—the longer term aspect of a travel event (as compared to other client events) permits for more complete educational and personal development opportunities, especially with special guests and authors available, and somewhat "captive".

The travel industry does a particularly good job of communicating not only the important information and details for the participants, but of generating anticipation and excitement. In addition to invitations, brochures and tickets sent, the host will certainly want to include additional communication pieces, and other touches, with the process: perhaps an agenda of planned activities, such as seminar content or a speaker's biography, for example, or providing group luggage tags, or commemorative badges, t-shirts or hats. The time-frames for communicating will almost certainly be extended, beginning with an early buzz, and prospective guests will require ample lead-time before making an RSVP commitment.

In many ways, travel events shine most brightly as creators of *lasting memories;* they are, perhaps, unique in their ability to provide the means for relationship-building, personal connections and a shared history. Picture taking, videos and group portraits are obvious pursuits, while *personally* autographed books become a much more feasible option, and meaningful keepsakes and souvenirs are more readily available. As well, the opportunity presents itself to address the group, at the end of the adventure, with a heartfelt and meaningful message of thanks, and acknowledgements: perhaps even referencing the trip-highlights and humerous foibles, relating to the experiences of the participants as individually as is practical.

I would be remiss were I not to point out that travel events come with additional risks to the organizer. You will almost certainly come to know some of your relationships better, and some of what you may learn you may not like. If you are gifted with patience and a relatively easy going personality, can manage your own expectations effectively, and can remember that many others possess none of these qualities, you are more likely to benefit greatly from these experiences. As well, if you should suffer from your own short-comings and "bad habits", it is more likely that others will learn of these while travelling and you will need to manage that accordingly. Adaption, differentiation, and the potential results requires just that sort of risk, however, and being prepared to do that which others are not prepared to do will continue to separate the successful from the less so.

A travel experience can transform the traveler. The *lasting memory* for the participant of a travel client event may be in the form of personal growth, or a new found appreciation for and understanding of a people, or country, a region, a culture, or even themselves. Again, the medium, the effort, the event itself, is part of the message to the guests; as with the Jane Goodall event, circumstances may conspire and the message may be much more lasting than planned and expected. Recently, I had been treated to just such an experience.

I had sequestered myself to work on this book, by embarking on a longish Mediterranean cruise, with a six day transatlantic crossing. Joined only by wife-and-dedicated-travel-partner, Anna, I enjoyed plenty of time by the pool, writing, and getting to know some of the staff. It was, by and large, a fairly typical, self-indulgent, hedonistic and frivolous journey dedicated to relaxation and peace, with no apparent effort on my part towards betterment. However, as the ship was nearing the final port in North America, the cruise director stood at the centre of the main stage, surrounded by staff of various colours, sizes and ethnicities, representing myriad nations, and offered a most interesting perspective; the essence of that message was:

Here are the people that worked together for this journey, to make the experience safe and enjoyable for all of us. They represent many countries, religions and cultures, but, they work together towards a common objective. Though the world seems to be filled with people that do not all get along or respect each other, we are proof that such people can live in peace and harmony.

His message was most sincere. Cruising is not about hedonism after all. It is about promoting world peace. I like that.

TREND: LEGACY

As baby boomers continue to age, and as they complete the transition from a life that has featured responsibilities and employment to a lifestyle that emphasizes leisure pursuits, new interests and desires will emerge. If we can summarize the motivation and efforts relative to the preparation for this recent transition with the phrase "preparing for retirement", then I suggest that a useful phrase to describe the motivation and efforts for the next transition will be "preparing a legacy".

Even with the current life expectancy, baby boomers will soon need to accept and address their mortality. They will wonder: what am I leaving behind? How will I be remembered? Opportunities will arise for business people, professionals and entrepreneurs to respond to these interests with products and services, for related purposes, and with specific processes. I expect we will also increasingly see these interests reflected in the planning of awesome client events. Although, admittedly, the legacy theme may not be as jubilantly obvious as those related to retirement, leisure and travel.

One of the more subtle, legacy-related approaches to awesome client events is through the inclusion of a featured charity, not-for-profit or foundation (hereinafter simply referred to as charity). Such an inclusion may contribute considerably to the overall relationship-building objectives, and provide for interesting opportunities related to the four key components.

Regarding participants, a charity client event with a strong and sincere fundraising effort, may attract the attention of a potentially large number of participants. In addition to the existing clients, partners and identified prospects, a host of unidentified prospects may be drawn to the venue and activity specifically because it is a fundraiser. The organization receiving the donations and proceeds may be inclined to promote the event to their own base of relationships, and the media may be more inclined to take notice and report the happenings as news. As a good and generous "citizen", the hosting business people or professionals may also gain general benefits related to public relations and branding, in support of other objectives, such as recruiting and human resource needs.

An organizer of charity events may also discover that some of the services they require, and for which they may have paid handsomely were it a regular client event, may be received at a considerably reduced cost (or no cost at all). Suppliers, printers, entertainers, speakers, etc., may be moved to provide their products and services at a discount in an effort to produce greater proceeds for the charity.

Sponsors and partners may also underwrite some of the related costs, or use the event as an opportunity to publically contribute to the featured charity, and thereby contribute significantly to the success of the event.

A number of years ago, for example, I organized a client, charity event in support of a rather unusual fundraising endeavor for ALS Canada. The featured effort with the fundraising was a climb of Mt Kilimanjaro by a group of financial services professionals, including a close associate. With the help of my brother-in-law, and event enthusiast, Chef Carlo, I was able to secure a reduced rate for the venue, food and refreshments. The featured and draw speaker, a local celebrity business person, had (thankfully) decided to waive a $10,000 fee (to support the charity). This inspired a significant corporate sponsor to match his "gift" with an equal, cash donation, and ultimately helped to attract the local media, which covered much of the fundraising activities, and mountain summit.

Charitable client events also present the opportunity to effectively combine both passive and interactive elements for the guests. Silent auctions and the regular, not-so-silent, auctions can be fun, inexpensive to organize, and valuable for the charity, while providing the participants with a lively and potentially memorable activity (especially if they are successful with their bids). Entertainers may be inclined to donate their talents, to round off the event experience, and these need not necessarily be purely passive.

As is typical of charity events, although clients, friends and family were invited, each is expected to purchase their own tickets in support of the charity. The value of the experience to the guests is in the organization of the event, the opportunity to enjoy some unusual and memorable experiences, while supporting an excellent cause.

While the inclusion of a fundraising initiative and support of a charity can contribute to the success of a client event, and the relationship-building objectives, some care and forethought must be exercised by the organizers. For example, I have witnessed some half-hearted, ad hoc attempts at including a charitable element to an event planning process; the worst of these seems to be when concerns about poor attendance arise, or an attempt is being made to attract sponsorship dollars and support. Events that feature charities should clearly be about the charity: first, last and always. The client relationship-building opportunity will come from the planner's sincerity about, and commitment to, that cause; relationships could just as easily be strained (or worse) when insincerity becomes apparent.

An interesting challenge may arise for the event hosts in the selection of the charity. With so many hopeful would-be beneficiaries, how can one choose whom to support? It may be that some tragedy befalls the organizer, or one of their positive relationships, and an emotion-fueled commitment to a cause results. With so many relationships to manage, however, it is most likely that a number of such tragedies may occur, and the hosts may feel pressure to address a growing (and endless) list of worthy organizations with support. As such, I think there is, perhaps, some merit to indentifying one or two such causes, and provide consistent support over time. The charitable event organizer may benefit from a long association with that organization, and from the knowledge that their support will become more significant and meaningful.

In some instances, a relationship-building business owner or professional will become associated with a particular cause or charity by virtue of an association with a collective, company, or professional organization. It is not uncommon, for example, that a financial services firm will support a charity "institutionally", or "at the corporate level" with a local fundraising activity, or even a national program. As such, financial services professionals connected with the firm might have the opportunity to add their own relationship-building effort within the structure of a larger event: "personalizing" the activities with their own contribution (and four key components) as part of a larger, more generic, initiative. While that professional may benefit from leveraging the greater efforts regarding that charity (larger events, public and media participation, interactive and passive elements, *lasting memories* components, etc), a risk is incurred that the firm, organization or collective ceases to support, or participate with, that charity in the future, and traction behind a long-term commitment may be jeopardized.

A particularly interesting opportunity may arise for an event enthusiast where the potential beneficiary of the fundraising effort is closely associated with a physical location. These maybe museums, historical sites, galleries, etc, that may also serve as suitable non-traditional venues for an activity. Such circumstances can provide a further feature of tangibility to the participants, as they can directly and immediately appreciate the potential value and benefits associated with the intended recipient of their generosity. As the legacy trend progresses among baby boomers, such events may evolve into grand affairs, where wealthier patrons are bequeathing a significant endowment.

Many professionals, including realtors, lawyers, accounts, investment advisors and financial planners, are anticipating significant business opportunities from the inter-generational transfer of wealth that is expected to occur as baby boomers pass away. These professionals may find that, by hosting client events, they will have the ability to meet, and build relationships with the inheriting generation. Indeed, specific activities could be developed to address related and important topics: such as estate planning or business succession planning. However, some creativity may be called for in the presentation of information on the topics to ensure that the event does not devolve into a sales pitch for a product or service. One way of approaching this might be with a cruise featuring (and jointly organized by) professionals addressing various issues related to succession planning with primarily self-employed clients (and their would-be successors) as participants.

Rather than the passing on of financial considerations, or other resources, a very different form of legacy activity may occur: the passing on of family-based memories, history and traditions. This potential trend could inspire content for events (a speaker on the topic of genealogy, tartans, or crests, for example) and for activities (such as an extended-family group travel). For those business owners and professionals that serve a particular ethnic group, relationship-building inspiration may come from that group's ethnic or cultural heritage. For example, an event organizer could target a few generations of a smaller number of families with a culinary experience featuring food and wine of their homeland, or/and with a particularly appropriate venue, such as a gallery with a collection of works from artists associated with their country of origin. As well, an organizer might take advantage of a particular entertainer, performance, or production that is closely associated with a tradition or culture (Fiddler on the Roof, for example) for a group of clients to whom that performance would have special meaning.

Though referred to simply as the *baby boom*, it is a mistake to think of that rise in population as being solely about North American's having had lots of babies. A statistically significant aspect of that boom had to do with immigration, and primarily from Europe. One might imagine, then, that a legacy trend in *our* aging population may be related to that immigration experience: a multi-generational travel event to reconnect to the language and culture of a homeland, for example, may have appeal. A few years ago, I had the opportunity to participate with a group of Italian immigrants, and their adult children, from Southern Ontario, on a bus trip to New York City. There the group visited Ellis Island, and the Immigration Museum, where they conducted research on their family—searching records for names, dates, etc. Much more than a mere holiday, this journey saw one generation remembering and learning about their own life, so that the next generation could also be aware, and appreciate the challenges, struggles and risks endured. It was about sharing an important history, adding to a story of a family, and contributing to a legacy.

CLASSIC EVENTS

Law

Very consistently, client events seem to reflect the personality and values of the organizers, and of the character of their industry or profession. To the layperson, the profession of law, for example, is often associated with a mood or atmosphere of seriousness and formality. Yet, even in that no nonsense environment, relationships are formed and then nurtured over time.

Frank P. Layton, Q.C., described to me the approach taken regarding relationship-building at the Edmonton office of one of Canada's most prestigious law firms, Bennett Jones. In his capacity as Managing Partner, Layton combined his leadership role and practice responsibilities with an enthusiastic support of their awesome client events.

In that interview, I came to appreciate some of the special challenges that may be faced by top-performing firms in that profession. Bennett Jones, for example, provides a wide range of specialty services, with expertise in a variety of topics, for an equally diverse group of clients that are successful, and very busy, in a dynamic global economy. Unlike the smaller scale, relative simplicity, and homogenous client profile often experienced by businesses, Layton and his associates would work with large corporate and government organizations, as well as icons from the world of sports and entertainment; they would endeavor to infuse the complex realm of international law with the "old fashioned values" and personalized service that constitutes the heritage of Bennett Jones.

Typical of their style, the firm had recently organized a banquet and dance. Guests were treated to a gourmet meal, refreshments and the entertainment of a full orchestra. The hosts combined a friendly and fun atmosphere with black-tie formality. The Hotel MacDonald is a favorite venue in Edmonton for such events. Located in the city's heart, the historic landmark offers an elegant atmosphere, fine catering, and suitable formal banquet facilities. Since some guests would be travelling to Edmonton specifically for the event, this traditional venue would also provide the added benefit of excellent accommodations.

The guests were primarily existing clients, although specific prospects and prominent citizens would also be invited. Lawyers from the firm were to submit a list of potential participants from their client base, with consideration given to venue capacity, and travel arrangements. The lists would then be compared in search of duplications, before implementing an involved communications process. Formal invitations were created "in house" and sent with a request to RSVP. To build excitement, and ensure that the participant's full attention had been gained, several communications were sent, in progressive fashion, with each more elaborate than the previous. If required, follow-up calls were also made to encourage participation and field any questions. During the event, Layton addressed the audience, offered sincere thanks, and build some *lasting memories.*

Dentistry

Also leaders in their field, Dentists Cameron and David Maclean have taken an approach to relationship building that seems to reflect their professional philosophy. Considering their clients as "whole persons" (and not just a mouth), the doctors address their needs, motives, values and over-all well being prior to co-creating health goals and action plans. They also consider the impact of their practice on the community, and want to contribute to the lives of others (even if they are not clients).

Working with the rest of their team at Dorchester Health Centre, and a host of like-minded, mostly health-related professionals, the doctors organized a large event featuring world-renowned speaker and author, Dr Deepak Chopra. The evening began with a private VIP reception, for specific guests, to meet Chopra; this included refreshments and the opportunity to have gifted books personally autographed. Following the reception, the VIP group joined approximately 2000 additional participants (including the general public) for Chopra's keynote presentation; referred to by Time Magazine as one of the Top 100 Icons and Heroes of the century, he shared his fascinating blend of Eastern Tradition philosophy with Western Tradition medicine. The two-hour presentation was punctuated by a twenty minute break to allow participants the opportunity to attend the mini trade show featuring the products and services of the event partners. All of the activities took place at Calgary's Telus Convention Centre: the keynote in the large, conference room, the VIP reception two floors up, and the trade show in the foyer.

A professional events coordinator brought together the team of sponsors, partners and other stakeholders for the elaborate client/ public event. Tickets sales were promoted by the team to their data base of positive relationships, and, with some media support, brisk ticket sales also occurred to unidentified prospects and the public. The doctors were recognized for their leadership at the event (to a very large audience), and a program with a description of their professional services was provided to all in attendance.

The event provided some significant contributions to *lasting memories:* ticket stubs and programs, autographed books, pictures with the draw speaker, products from the vendors, and for some the words of Deepak Chopra would be potentially life-changing.

CHARITABLE EVENTS

Las Vegas Gala for Breast Cancer

When compared to typical client events, those that feature fundraising objectives seem to benefit from unusual, creative and memorable combinations of passive and interactive elements. Over the past ten years, I have attended, and contributed to, many such events, but a few stand out.

Connie Hamilton, for example, was a team leader in a national direct sales organization of the fashion industry: providing fashion coordination for her female clients, and assisting the members of her team as they built their own businesses. Through her own style of awesome client events, she pursued her mission to engender self-confidence to her teammates and clients, and to extend that spirit beyond her regular business activity. This included fundraising for breast cancer research.

The event was promoted as a "Las Vegas Style Gala". The evening began with a cocktail reception, and silent auction, hosted by an appropriately attired "Las Vegas showgirl"; a full banquet followed, with entertaining presentations from corporate sponsors. After dinner, the Vegas theme continued with a full orchestra, a very talented jazz vocalist, and a mock casino (with many enthusiastic participants). Proceeds from the silent auction and event ticket sales were donated to the featured charity.

A centrally located restaurant was selected as the venue; its unique, three-story lay-out provided an exceptional environment for mingling and interaction. The bottom floor held the banquet, stage, dance floor and silent auction, while the middle floor held several gaming tables, main bar and smoker's lounge, and the top floor was home to craps tables and a martini bar.

Connie and her team organized the event primarily for their clients, who were encouraged to bring spouses and friends. Other participants included many corporate and individual sponsors, event partners and contributors of cash, talent and silent auction donations.

Participation was encouraged through invitations (sent well in advance), requesting an RSVP, and instructing to order tickets. Representatives of the charity, and key organizers, took many opportunities to acknowledge the attendees and contributors, and provide thanks for the support. All guests were provided with gift certificates, and tickets to another up-coming event, while the more diligent and committed participants in the silent auction secured their own special keepsakes.

Hypno Show for Special Olympics

A second, very memorable event was highlighted with the guests volunteering to be part of the entertainment. Faith Wood, a well-known hypnotist and entertainer, and former law enforcement professional, organized a fundraising activity for the Law Enforcement Torch Run (in support of Special Olympics).

In addition to an engaging silent auction, the draw activity for the event was a stage show featuring Faith's talents as a hypnotist, and the willingness of some of those in the audience to participate. The show was family orientated, and designed to ensure that neither those on stage nor in the audience would be embarrassed or uncomfortable. A representative from the charitable organization also provided a brief, but moving, presentation and video.

Participation was generated through invitations, posters, tickets and a promotional campaign directed at associated groups, and friends, family and associates of the organizers. Faith's reputation for lively fundraising, and history of commitment to the community, was instrumental in generating attendance. I treated the activity as a form of client event, and personally encouraged participation among my own base of positive relationships. A number of other event partners contributed silent auction items, and distributed tickets.

The show itself was very memorable for audience (though it is hard to say what those hypnotized might recall), and a video recording was produced for *lasting memories,* business branding, and additional fundraising efforts.

Balloon Castle for Local Library

Many of the professionals I have met and worked with seemed to be blessed with many skills and talents. As such, opportunities may arise for the host to contribute his or her talents as an aspect of the passive or interactive components of an event. While some additional cost savings may be realized, the real benefit may come as the audience—the guests—experience a different, perhaps more artistic, side of their financial advisor, realtor, accountant, etc.

I believe it is fairly widely accepted, for example, that President Bill Clinton's saxophone performance of *Heartbreak Hotel* (while wearing sunglasses), or Prime Minister Stephen Harper's piano and vocal performance of *With a Little Help From My Friends,* both on national television, contributed positively to their over-all image.

Recently I attended a community fundraiser event as a guest, with the organizing professional also participating as the featured entertainment. The host was a young accountant, in early stages of business building: working hard to brand himself in his community, and keen on attracting new relationships.

The venue for the event, and beneficiary of the fundraising and community awareness efforts, was a local public library. The young professional and his associates had constructed a castle and waterfall out of balloons, and suspended from the ceiling was an impressive flying dragon—also made from balloons. The castle served as a play area for the countless young readers that visited the library over the course of the weekend, and also doubled as a stage from which the accountant and his team provided a magic and juggling act to the delight of the entranced young audience.

Though intended for the library and children, the professionals were of course introduced to all of the parents, community leaders and stakeholders, and sponsoring organizations. As well, the highly visual nature of the performance and balloon staging lent itself well to many photo opportunities, which local media eagerly seized!

I am proud to report the business person behind this particular event, and one of the performers, was my son, Chris.

MOCK ADVENTURES

Destination Africa

An event that encourages, or even requires, movement, interaction, and engagement for the participants can be most effective for memory-making and relationship-building; some imagination, however, on the part of the organizers may be required, as well as on the part of the guests.

Having held a few successful client events at the Calgary Zoo, my team and I watched patiently, and with great curiosity, as the new and exciting Destination Africa attractions were being built. Though located on an island in the Bow River, near the centre of Calgary, and immediately adjacent to busy transportation arteries, most of the zoo is hidden from view from the passing commuters. An exception became the tall glass spire from one of these new buildings, emerging over tree—tops, and gaining the attention the public.

Three buildings in all were created as part of the very significant expansion to the zoo: an African Savannah exhibit, an African Rain

Forest exhibit, and a large African-themed reception hall. The media had been reporting the progress, and considerable public buzz had been established before a select group (including myself) was invited to the grand opening celebration. Soon after, I and my team organized our own Destination Africa event for clients and special guests.

We were able to secure the envelopes and invitations that had been designed and printed especially for the grand opening and then personalized them for our own private event. The *adventure* occurred after regular park hours, which established an appropriate air of exclusivity for the guests. Upon entering the extensive zoo grounds, attendees were directed to the newly-constructed facilities.

The event began in the central African reception hall, where I provided a few words of introduction, acknowledgements, thanks and a description of the evening's agenda. I described the featured activity: guests would be divided up into four groups, and provided a behind-the-scenes tour of the new savannah and rainforest exhibits by an experienced guide. As well, the guests were encouraged to participate in a form of scavenger hunt: completing a nature quiz by looking for answers that could be found on their safari. To encourage their natural curiosity along, guests were promised a prize for completing the quiz.

After the tour, all were reassembled in the main hall for finger food, wine, mingling, and a few more words of thanks by yours truly.

Vine Dining

As I was busy trying to build a successful financial planning practice in Calgary, an old childhood friend, Lawrence Franco, was busy climbing the corporate ladder in Toronto. Though our business environments were often profoundly different, we have shared the same need to attract and maintain superior relationships.

During his years in senior management for Dun and Bradstreet Canada, Franco participated in the organization and hosting of a variety of awesome client events, including one of my favorite mock adventures: *vine dinning*.

Festivities took place at Chateau Des Charmes—a winery near Ontario's beautiful Niagara-On-The-Lake. The venue was selected in part because of its attractive and accommodating vineyard, and in part because of its proximity to a conference at which many attendees were Dun and Bradstreet clients.

These attendees were enticed away from the conference by a creative communications strategy. The official conference program promoted the event, creating a suitable buzz, and the follow-up invitations were appropriately in the form of corkscrews and wine bottles—with the event details presented on the bottle's label.

Guests were escorted to the vineyard by shuttle bus, and treated to a memorable dinning experience; strategically located throughout the grounds were various buffet style stations featuring different culinary traditions and styles, including Italian, seafood, vegetarian, and dessert. As expected, stations included a selection of wines to compliment the dishes.

As guests wandered and mingled from station to station, they were also delighted by different forms of entertainment; they could listen to music, have their picture drawn (as a caricature), and even have their handwriting analyzed. The analysis, caricature, and corkscrew invitations were kept by the guests, and became part of the event's *lasting memories.*

Franco's relationship-building skills—honed at Dun and Bradstreet—seems to have served him well, as he has continued to ascend the corporate ladder.

Adventures in Retirement

Not long after the publication of the original Awesome Client Events, I received a request from a group of investment advisors in Lethbridge, Alberta, to assist them with the planning and hosting of a client event.

I was particularly intrigued by the request, as the advisors had recently completed a transition to a new dealership: CIBC Wood Gundy. As such, they were feeling a special need to connect with their clients—many of whom had transitioned to the new firm as well.

Together, we conceptualized a rather ambitious and unusual event based upon an inspiring theme, *adventures in retirement.*

The event took place on a Saturday afternoon, at a large airplane hangar, at the regional airport, on the edge of the city. In the middle of the hangar, a lunch buffet was provided, with refreshments that included a selection of wine.

At one end of the hangar was a large door, which would normally accommodate the entrance and exit of the plane. The door was ajar, and provided the guests access to the adventures in retirement business fair. This fair featured the kinds "toys" that successful retirees might aspire to own, in pursuit of their life's last adventures. There was a touring motorcycle, a classic themed sports car, a boat, a large motor home, and even a small private jet! The guests were encourage to get in, try out, explore, and even just sit on, the various "toys", while a dutiful photographer was capturing pictures. These products, as well as the hangar itself, were provided by businesses that were clients and associates of the investment advisors— eager to have an opportunity to promote their own businesses to the guests.

At the other end of the hangar was small door that lead out of the building, to a run way, and a small plane—owned by the company that provided the venue. On this plane, guests were taken on a brief flight around the city, and back to the event.

At mid afternoon, the guests were invited to the centre of the hangar for a short motivational keynote delivered by me, and a series of heart-felt acknowledgements and thanks from the hosting advisors.

ACTION EVENTS

───────── ✤ ─────────

Some professions are more obviously associated with physical excursion than others. Entrepreneurs and innovators dedicated to personal training, physiotherapy, chiropractic, and sports medicine, for example, have provided stellar examples of client events; for these, the inclusion of memory-making activity within relationship building strategies seems to occur naturally.

Dr. Chris Oswald is a clear leader in this category, and has continued to be an inspiration and trend-setter throughout his career. My introduction to his successful chiropractic practice, personal brand, and awesome client events, occurred as I was planning my own initial events, and just getting a glimpse of the potential of the strategy. At that time, a notable event for Dr Oswald, and his associate Dr Lewis, was described as "extreme mountain biking".

The primary activity of this event was a day of cycling through the wilderness of southern Ontario over physically challenging terrain, which concluded with a well-earned barbeque feast and drinks. The doctors selected a conservation area where biking enthusiasts had forged single-track trails and which provided a degree of difficulty known to be suitable for the cyclists.

Existing clients, associates, and friends were invited verbally (to gauge interest) and then formally by a written invitation (which included a description of activities, directions, and a request to RSVP). During the barbeque, participants were warmly addressed by the hosts, and the event's success was shared, by the practice newsletter, with the many more relationships that did not attend.

Lasting memories of the event were promoted by group pictures, which were eventually distributed by newsletter, and framed and prominently displayed in the physical premises: a reminder to the participants of the relationship, an encouragement of future participation, and a clever demonstration of the culture and novelty of the practice to potential new relationships.

Over the years, Dr Oswald has continued with his pursuit of excellence in many aspects of his professional endeavors, including those with respect to client events. In more recent years, relationship-building activities have become more ambitious, and have taken him and his colleagues to more exotic destinations, like the South of France.

Participants are invited to Provence, and to *echappee en velo*— escape on your bike. The adventure unfolds over several days of preparation and cycling through the French countryside, with rejuvenation available at charming accommodations along the way. The activities include ample opportunity for fun a personal growth through interaction with specialists in health, lifestyle, nutrition and culinary arts.

Potential guests are sourced from the extensive network of relationships associated with Dr Oswald and several event partners. The communications efforts include hard copy and soft copy post cards and brochures to existing clients and identified prospects. Unidentified prospects are sourced through various referral relationships and web-based initiatives.

These travel events have become just one element of Dr Oswald's extraordinary business operations, which have grown well beyond the services often associated with chiropractic to include writing, teaching, and health care products. The objective, he reports, is to inspire in his clients the "faith, confidence and belief that we are leaders in our field". I am definitely a believer.

RETIRE TO MEXICO!

Many of the events that I have planned, hosted and participated in have tended to have an element of adventure. Initially, the guests and other participants were invited to experience these vicariously through the lives and stories of others. Gradually, the guests became more actively engaged in these pursuits; though not quite fully becoming the adventurer during the event, they were least being pointed in a direction and nudged along, towards some fulfilling life experience.

This trend ultimately manifested in the real client event adventures that were organized as part of our relationship building efforts with *Canadians Retiring Abroad.*

The company was formed by a small group of professionals to provide accounting and financial planning support for Canadians seeking to have an international retirement experience. Motivated by our early success with these efforts, I convinced the team that we were in a position to set a higher standard for client events, and actually plan events in the retirement destinations that we were of interest to the clients. Rather than merely showing videos and pictures of the expatriate communities popular among Canadians, we would plan and host events that combined education with vacation.

The first of these was organized as a cruise. Sailing in and out of California, the stops included Puerto Vallarta, Mazatlan and Cabo San Lucus. During the mornings of the days at sea, members of our team provided lectures for our guests in a conference room provided by the cruise line. The classes covered some the key topics normally of interest to the prospective snowbirds and expats: tax, residency, banking, health care, lifestyle, real estate, cost of living, etc. We were able to entice a guest speaker and author, with a free cruise, to provide a special keynote presentation, and signed copies of his book, Mazatlan Is Paradise.

During a couple of the days in port, we planned our own group excursion to not only see some tourist sites, but to see where and how the Canadian retirees live in the gringo communities of Mexico's west coast. Though participation in the excursions was at the option of our guests, all were eager to participate.

Evenings back on the ship provided ample opportunity for relationship building, typically over dinner and drinks. We, as hosting professionals, were happy to share information with our existing and prospective clients, while they were happy to pick our brains and receive guidance in a relaxed environment, and without worrying about billable hours.

Subsequent *Retire to Mexico!* events took place at all-inclusive resorts. The first of these—by popular demand—was in Mazatlan. As with the cruise, all guests stayed at the same resort, and morning lectures were provided by the hosting team of professionals. Excursions were also planned to assist the attendees with their experience of the community, and, especially, to introduce them to the retirement lifestyle of the many Canadian snowbirds enjoying Mexico.

These travel client events have come to form many of my fondest work-related memories. All participants—the existing and prospective clients, the professional team, and my family—were all brought closer together by the shared life experiences. Whether or not anyone eventually chose to "retire to Mexico" was ultimately relatively unimportant; the objective was to attract and retain superior relationships.

Some of these relationships were attracted to the event out of a mutual desire: to pursue personal goals related to travel. For many professionals and business owners, still actively building their business, this common interest among their clients will be a trend that can be tapped into for years to come. In the planning and hosting of the educational vacations, we also witnessed the emergence of the legacy trend among many of these baby boomers, as some purchased a recreational property in one of the Mexican communities visited.

Explaining their motivation, the purchasers reported that the property would be enjoyed together with friends and family, and then passed on to the next generation.

CONCLUSION

THE ART OF WAR

I f the importance and quality of an idea can be measured by the length of time over which mankind has sought its application, then those ideas associated with *The Art of War* must be among our most significant. With the notable exception of literature associated with a religion, this collection of prescriptions is arguably without equal as a guide employed across cultures and geography, and in various situations and context.

Long before I studied finance and investing, I was a student of philosophy, and was introduced to the wisdom traditions of Asia, including *The Art of War*. I was practical, and believed that the study of these traditions would be useful, not only academically (as preparation for law school), but as preparation for life.

As it turned out, the life I prepared for has been one of competition, and an on-going desire for self-improvement and success. *The Art of War* has been one of the texts that I have returned to over the years to assist me with these pursuits—even with respect to relationship-building and client events. Though, I confess, I have found that its wisdom is not given up easily, and it took several attempts before I was able to distill its message to a core of precepts:

Know Your Competition
Know Yourself
Know the Weather
Know the Terrain

Know Your Competition/Know Yourself

The translation of an ancient text, that was originally presented in a very foreign language and writing form, would permit generous license to the translator. The first precept of *The Art of War*, for example, is often presented as "know your enemy". From a contemporary perspective, it is far more useful to think of our "enemy" more broadly (and more gently) as our "competition".

As professionals, entrepreneurs, and business people, we should understand the competitors in our field. To "know" them is to come to understand their features. Are they large, or small? Are they intricate, structured and resourceful? To begin, the features are more or less objective. It does not necessarily follow from the fact that a competitor is large, that it is also strong, for example. Indeed, the size of a competitor may suggest that it is firm and stable, or that it is entrenched, rigid, or brittle.

These features are also relative. They are relative to our own conditions. Therefore, to truly know and understand our competitors, we must "know ourselves". In comparison with the competition, are we large or small, resourceful or underfunded, innovative or old-fashioned? When understanding ourselves or our competitors, there are no absolute strengths and weakness, there are only relative strengths and weaknesses. Moreover, these strengths and weaknesses are the result of perspective and based upon opinion; they are subjective.

As such, our condition, relative to our competitor, is never entirely negative or entirely positive; it is merely different. And, as I have suggested throughout this book, from this difference, and from the ability to differentiate, opportunities emerge.

In the financial services industry, and professions of law, real estate and accounting, for example, there are large and well-known organizations. Their resources are significant and their brands formidable. Were they to set their minds to the creation of relationship-building client events, they would have abilities far beyond those available to smaller organizations. However, supposed strengths can quickly become weaknesses, if their competitors make it so. When we know our competitor and know ourselves, we can then determine what alterations or improvements can be made to gain some advantage. What smaller organizations may lack in resources, they may gain in flexibility, maneuverability, and speed. This insight can be very useful when developing a culture of relationship-building through awesome client events in your businesses or practice.

During my tenure in the financial services industry, I have been involved with a wide array of companies and organizations, differing by various measures. Generally speaking, I have experienced an inverse correlation between the size of the organization, and the ability of the members to be risk takers. I have also come to feel that risk taking can be an important ingredient in client events. Very recently, I made a conscious decision to take a calculated risk with respect to a client event, and in that I am part of a comparatively small organization, I was able to take that risk.

The participants of the event included consumers of financial services products, some of our corporate team, the community at large, and, importantly, an identified group of prospective new advisors and a product partners. The objective of the event was to not only build on the current relationships, and initiate some new relationships, but in particular, to introduce the prospective new advisors and product partners to the culture of our organization. I wanted to clearly indicate that we were different, perhaps even creative.

The venue for the event was a Buddhist Temple in the local community. It is the kind of interesting building that one drives by regularly and wonders what goes on inside, and I anticipated that this curiosity would be an important draw for guests. The emcee for the event was the Sensai for the temple, James Martin, who provided the guests with an introduction to the temple and traditions associated with his sect of Buddhism. I provided a lively keynote presentation on the topic of ethics, social responsibility, and investing entitled: "Where Does the Money Go?" Not only was this topic appropriate for the venue, but I knew in advance that many of the identified prospects had an interest in the subject matter as well.

The communications strategy included an invitation and ticket campaign, which were designed and organized by my daughter, Jessica. These were distributed in hard and soft copy to the identified prospects, some existing clients, and select members of our corporate team. As the event was also of general interest to the community of Buddhists associated with temple, they saw it as a public relations opportunity, and were happy to promote the event as well.

As the event was being organized, and the participants were being communicated to, I began to receive some feedback from a few colleagues and associates. The sentiment could be summarized as primarily negative; my judgment regarding the attractiveness of the topic, and the appropriateness of the venue, given the stereotypical conservatism of the community, was being politely questioned. Indeed, I began to have doubts myself. My vindication came on the night of the event with an attendance of more than twice the number hoped, and which left stragglers standing at the back.

I am pleased to have been in a position to take a risk with the event.

Though not every risk produces the desired results, the unusual success of memorable events does not typically result without some risk. Many of the larger financial institutions, with whom our organization completes, would be unlikely or simply unable to offer the same sort of client experience.

Over the years, I have come to know my competition and come to know myself. This empowers me to compete by focusing my efforts on what I can do well, and they cannot.

Know the Weather/Know the Terrain

As I apply *The Art of War* to my modern experience of competition, I interpret the terms *weather* and *terrain* to mean *variables*.
To "know the weather" is to identify and understand the variables
that we **cannot** control.

The weather is the *stuff* that happens while we are competing: the
elements that contribute to the dynamism of the environment, the
constancy of change. While we cannot control these variables, and
cannot consistently forecast their occurrence and impact, we can
prepare. To "know the weather" is to identify the changes that may
happen, and prepare a contingency plan. It is also to understand
and accept that change will most certainly happen, and that if your
ability to compete is dependent upon a static environment, you will
almost certainly face significant challenges eventually.

Perhaps your business is strongly associated with, or heavily relies
on, a of set conditions: a rising stock market, or low interest rates,
or a stable housing market, or current tax laws, or a generous health
care system, or the availability of credit, or a strong economy, or
the popularity of a particular treatment, or the reputation of your
sponsor firm, etc. If the continued success, or even the viability, of
your business is reliant upon these conditions, and if these conditions are variables that you cannot control, then you are exposed to
risk as the inevitable changes unfold.

To "know the terrain" is to come to understand the variables that
you **can** control in the course of competition. It is to determine
where and when to engage in battle. If we "know our competition"

and "know ourselves", and we ascertain the relative strengths and weaknesses, then we can determine what conditions present the best opportunity to capitalize on our strengths and best exploit their weaknesses. This is *where* we do battle; it is the *terrain* that we will seek.

Can you execute your business in a way that makes your success more reliant upon the variables that you can control, rather than the variables that you cannot control?

In my case, I found that, while I had virtually no influence over the many causes and conditions that impact the performance and popularity of the myriad products and services of the financial services sector, I could certainly influence the quality of the relationships that I enjoyed with the clients, partners, suppliers, etc. Awesome client events provide the means to help me make my business *about those relationships.*

These precepts—*know your competition, know yourself, know the weather,* and *know the terrain*—were guiding principles behind our team's most recent and, in some respects, most ambitious event.

COMMUNITY CULTURAL EVENT

✦

Canadian cities and communities amply reward its citizens for their endurance of the long, and often exhausting, winters with a generous offering of summer festivals and cultural events. Many of these are annual activities, with the attendance, attention and popularity growing each year—becoming tourist attractions, and institutions unto themselves. Such events begin with the ideas and efforts of someone, or some group. Over time, they become under the direction of significant organizations, with substantial budgets, and government, media and corporate relationships.

Inspired and motivated by my brother-in-law, Chef Carlo, and his success in becoming meaningfully involved with some of Calgary's most important annual events, I had long pondered how I might pursue such an opportunity, and how such an event or festival might become an element of a client event. After considerable reflection (and some coaching from Carlo), I concluded that the best opportunity to provide the most value to the organization of a festival, and the most opportunity for relationship-building, would come at the inception of the event, and its inauguration.

During the planning and execution of the event at the Buddhist Temple, I became aware of the interest of the Calgary Japanese Cultural Association in launching an annual summer festival in support of Japanese culture; I learned that summer is the traditional time for the celebration of family, through reunion, and the honouring of ancestors. In that I had been assessing venue opportunities throughout my local community, and was aware that a new park and community centre would make an ideal location for such an event, I volunteered to sit on the board of the organizing committee. My role on the board quickly expanded, as I offered to assist with sponsorship and communications strategy. I was able to leverage my pre-existing relationships in the local businesses community to quickly rally enthusiastic support for the proposed event.

A successful event was the positive goal of an ever-increasing number of stake holders and, as such, the number of positive relationships was growing rapidly. This suggested to me that the potential for a very significant number of participants was emerging, including clients, identified and unidentified prospects, members of my corporate team, event partners, the public and the media. The event partners came to include the Calgary Japanese Cultural Association, Calgary Buddhist Temple, and a number of local business owners, each with incentive to identify and communicate to their own members, customers, clients and other relationships.

The venue proved to be an ideal location for such a festival. In some respects, the park and community centre was traditional: centrally located, ample parking, adjacent to public transit, and providing all amenities. However, as a new facility, with a modern look and a beautiful park, the location would have been novel to most of the guests; even for the locals, the venue became non-traditional as it was transformed by decorations, music, and aromas into something far more foreign and exotic.

The festival included a variety of passive and interactive elements designed to attract and entertain guests of all ages and ethnicities for the entire day. An out-door stage featured a succession of Japanese artists and performers, including actors, dancers, various musicians, and martial artists. Periodically, traditionally costumed dancers circled the guest sitting area to perform a form of Japanese dance associated with *Obon*—which was the theme of the event. Guests were encouraged to participate in the circle and learn to dance as well. For those seeking a more physical exertion, there was a mock sumo wrestling area, where participants could wear special padded sumo suits and attempt to "wrestle" their friends. Inside the community centre, guests could wander and enjoy an extensive display of Japanese art and cultural artifacts. Guests eagerly purchased Japanese inspired food and refreshments—of which the "dharma dogs" were the most popular.

In addition to promoting Japanese culture, the purpose of the event was to provide an opportunity for members of the community to celebrate their own families. As such, traditional Japanese games for children were organized, as well as costumes and masks. My son, Chris, provided balloon animals from a booth sponsored by local businesses. Moreover, the park itself also sported a superb playground for those children with a little extra energy to burn.

The communications program included a variety of elements and unfolded for two months prior to the event. One of the unexpected pleasures of organizing this particular event was the involvement of my daughter, Jessica, who was instrumental in executing the communications strategy. Our first task was to raise funds to cover costs of promotion. Local businesses were solicited to make a modest sponsorship contribution, in exchange for credit and logo placement on advertisement and other promotional materials. In addition to the benefit of driving traffic and attention to the community, the businesses hoped to get in on the ground floor of an annual event. Some local print advertising was arranged to promote the event, but very colourful invitations, postcards and posters were also created. These were displayed and distributed throughout the community surrounding the festival's venue, as well as through other Japanese organizations and businesses throughout the city. All event stakeholders and partners were encouraged to generously share soft copy versions of the posters to all of their relationships, and to promote the event through existing on-line newsletters, websites and through social media. The entire hard cost of the communications campaign was approximately $1000.

This was to be the very first cultural event of its kind in the community, and the first attempt by the Calgary Japanese Community Association and Calgary Buddhist Temple at hosting a festival. As such, none of us had any idea as to the number of guests that would attend, but we had set a goal of 400 to 500. I think it is safe to say that absolutely everyone was extremely surprised by the enthusiastic turnout: estimated to have been approximately 1500! I was personally delighted to have been able to count many of those in attendance as my own relationships: my wife, children, clients, business associates, and their friends and family. I had also made a special effort to meet with, and personally invite, our local alderman (who was only recently elected); he graciously participated, addressed the audience, thanked the organizers, and had a videographer record some of the festivities.

Lasting memories were being promoted throughout the festival. While some left with decorative masks, fans and other keepsakes, others were captured by one or more of the wandering photographers and videographers—perhaps learning to dance, or to sumo. These images were quickly on their way to many of the guests by e-mail, as well as to newsletters, websites and other media. It is hoped that the event will not merely be relegated to memory, but that the festival will become an annual event—a legacy for the community—which will provide the opportunity for client events and relationship building for years to come.

ACKNOWLEDGEMENTS

Pick up a copy of *The Art of War* and typically you will see that Sun Tzu is credited as its "author". But as you learn more about the book, and its history, you may get the sense that it does not reflect the ideas of a single individual. Indeed, it may be that *The Art of War* was not "authored" at all, but represents a collection of ideas—of wisdom—that was accumulated over time, and contributed to by a great number of thinkers.

Similarly, *More Awesome Client Events* is the result of a number of contributors, whose stories and experiences are being gathered over time, and a growing number of participants, whose efforts are combined to produce memorable, relationship-building events. This is to thank and acknowledge some of the more significant of these:

Thanks to my wife, Anna; for your patience and constant support; you are a fantastic life and travel partner.

Thanks to my children, Chris and Jessica, for all of your help; I hope that these events were wonderful aspects of your childhood, and continue to be part of your life as you pursue your own success.

Thanks to my brother-in-law, Chef Carlo Cecchetto, for being entertaining, interesting and inspiring.

Thanks to the many friends and clients that attended the events; your participation, support and feedback has been essential.

Thanks to supportive colleagues and business associates, especially Rick Unrau, President of Global Exempt Market Solutions, Brian Mennis, Regional Director for Investors Group, and my partners at Canadians Retiring Abroad, Cam McIntosh and Dave Appleton.

Thanks to those that shared their talents to make the events a success: especially Jane Goodall, Brian Keating and Bruce Kirkby.

Thanks to the many generous top-performing professionals, who have shared their own stories of success, especially Dr Chris Oswald.

Thanks to Faith Wood for her feedback and mentorship regarding the production of this book.

ABOUT THE AUTHOR

Rod Burylo has worked throughout the financial services industry: as a banker and commission-based mortgage broker for Royal Bank, as a stock and options broker for Jones, Gable and Company, and as a financial advisor, trainer and manager for Investors Group.

After completing an undergraduate degree in Philosophy, Burylo completed various banking, insurance and investment designations and licenses, including that of Certified Financial Planner in 1997.

Burylo is a founding member of Canadians Retiring Abroad, recipient of the prestigious Advisor of the Year Award in 2004, and then served as Chief Compliance Officer for Global Exempt Market Solutions, a leading exempt market dealership.

Throughout is career, Burylo has contributed generously to the advancement of the financial services industry as a writer, educator, keynote speaker and volunteer. As well as a writer of books, he has been a columnist, contributor and professional source for newspapers and magazines throughout Canada. Burylo continues to serve in support of professional development organizations and associa-

tions, including Advocis and GAMA Canada, and provides training and lectures to audiences throughout North America.

When he is not working, Burylo is most likely to be travelling with his lovely wife, Anna.